Praise for
Talk to Me God, Before I Slap Somebody!

"You had me at the title: *Talk to Me God, Before I Slap Somebody!* However, I was truly sold after reading many of Renee's raw, real, revolutionary, life-altering stories, which gave me a fresh perspective on how God shows up—especially when we trust He will! Thanks to the story 'Go Ahead, Mock Me,' I now expect God to provide me a front parking space! Whether you do or don't know God already, you will be entertained and unable to put down this witty, yet inspiring read."

— ***Colleen McManus Lucksinger,***
Coach Coll Consulting, LLC, Joyful Connector!

⁂⁂⁂⁂

"When you pick up this book, you're not just getting stories—you're stepping into Reneé's life. And if you know her like I do, you know every word here is real. She's funny, bold, unfiltered, and sometimes a little wild—but always, always listening for the voice of God.

"*Talk to Me God, Before I Slap Somebody!* will make you laugh, maybe cry, and definitely think. In these pages you'll meet a woman who's walked through hard battles, crazy adventures, and moments that can only be explained as miracles. Through it all, Reneé shows us that God's voice isn't distant—it's personal, practical, and present in everyday life.

"Reading *Talk to Me God, Before I Slap Somebody!* is like sitting across the table with Reneé over coffee—except you don't have to brace yourself for her telling you exactly what she thinks (in love, of course). My hope is that as you read, you'll not just hear her stories but catch the invitation to hear God's voice in your own."

—*Sam Tichenor,* Worship Pastor of
New Life Ministries Endicott, New York

"There's a moment in every person's life where we are confronted with the realization if God is real. In Renee Budde's powerful new book, *Talk to me God, Before I Slap Somebody!* she brings the reader into the profound interchange of this reality. Her prose captivates every heart with sharp wit and humor and takes you on a wild ride into the miraculous. Taking you on a meandering path into God's world where real life stories come alive, you'll leave believing more and noticing more! This is for the hungry ones searching for REAL connections with God! You will laugh, cry, and ponder, never to be the same after spending time with Renee. With incredible testaments of God's love and redemption, this inspiring book will change you!"

— *Maria Sainz,* Senior Leader Red Seal Ministries,
San Diego, and author of *Miracles Still Happen*

"Authentic to who she is in person, Renee's flair flies off the page with grace; rambunctious humor; and well-timed, gut-punching truth. Her stories will make you laugh; some will cause you to cry, and page after page will bring you closer to the heart of God."

— *Evan Martin,* Lead Pastor, Colorado Church

✳✳✳✳

"Through a series of brief vignettes from her life's experience, the author takes us along on her journey from faith as an afterthought to faith as the core of her being. Reneé is a woman of wit and faith; both shine through these pages."

— *Lisa Hamilton-Fieldman*

Talk to Me God, Before I Slap Somebody!

Talk to Me God, Before I Slap Somebody!

A Personal Journey

Reneé Budde

MEDIA.COM

Talk to Me God,
Before I Slap Somebody!

Copyright © 2026 by Reneé Budde

Scripture verses marked NIV are taken from the Holy Bible, New International Version®, NIV® Copyright ©1973, 1978, 1984, 2011 by Biblica, Inc.® Used by permission. All rights reserved worldwide. Scripture verses marked ESV are taken from The ESV® Bible (The Holy Bible, English Standard Version®), © 2001 by Crossway, a publishing ministry of Good News Publishers. ESV Text Edition: 2025. Scripture verses marked NASB are taken from the New American Standard Bible®, Copyright © 1960, 1971, 1977, 1995, 2020 by The Lockman Foundation. All rights reserved. Scripture verses marked TLV are taken from the Tree of Life (TLV) Translation of the Bible. Copyright © 2015 by The Messianic Jewish Family Bible Society.

The views and opinions expressed in this book are those of the author and do not necessarily reflect the official policy or position of Illumify Media Global.

Published by
Illumify Media Global
www.IllumifyMedia.com
"Let's bring your book to life!"

Paperback ISBN: 978-1-964251-95-0

Cover design by Debbie Lewis

Front cover photo by Sunshine Underwood, Shiny Image LLC

Printed in the United States of America

To Bertha
an old, frail, Spirit led, praying woman I never met,
but who changed my life

Disclaimer Alert!

This book may bring out hostility, resentment,
and all that's ugly, in both you and me!
All the stories are unashamedly true.
For levity's sake, exaggerated descriptions such as
Judge,
or Snake Slayer are playfully inserted.

To know God, is to hear God.
God is full of surprises.
Grab what speaks to you.
Some aspects might need pondering
over tea or a shot of whiskey.

WARNING:
Raw. Real. Revolutionary.
Religious Perspectives Could Be Forever Altered!
Don't say I didn't warn you!

Contents

Introduction

Inquiring minds want to know:
What does the voice of God sound like?

God's voice is a thought that is not my own,
neither does it leave me.

Discover the voice for yourself.
Revelation is caught not taught.
Catch the revelation!
Change your life.

Look for the funny. Listen for the voice.
Transformation is inevitable if you're hungry.

This I promise,
You've NEVER read a book like this.

Battles are messy. Minefields are real. Brace for impact!

Unimaginable. Unforgettable. Priceless.

Grab a cup of coffee
Sit a spell
I have a few stories to tell

Lend me your ear
These are all true stories
I know you'll wanna hear

Of a lady on a mission
Not to be denied
Watch for amazing
To open up inside

FOUNDATIONS

"In the Garden,"
a simple church hymn of long ago
planted a seed:
"and He walks with me
and He talks with me
and He tells me, I am His own."
It sprouted, and I had the audacity to believe it!

Lyrics from "In the Garden" by C. Austin Miles (1912)

Passion

It's Tuesday morning before Thanksgiving. Should be twisting hair, but nooooo, sleep deprived, in front of the courtroom judge, I stand.

It's not every day one snaps. Passion is an odd sort. It's spicy. Intense. Flavored with spontaneity. Not all have it. Passion seasons life with intrigue and a splash of thrill.

Passion might resemble a feisty exchange no one saw coming in the ladies' room. A woman expressed her opinion over my recent decision to strut about shiny white hair over glaring faded roots.

"I preferred your hair colored."

Unretrievable words flew from loose lips: "If I slept with you, your opinion would matter."

I know. I can't believe it either. Not my proudest moment.

Don't judge me. You might have done the same.

Before forty, I was well behaved, compliant, and silent. A shrinking violet. Possibly not much different than yourself.

So, when my twenty-seven-year marriage erupted after suffering years of the silent treatment, someone was bound to be hurt or carted off in the paddy wagon.

Life wasn't always this volatile.

Talk to Me God, Before I Slap Somebody!

God, Are You Real?

Faith was not always a part of my life, but church attendance was. As a teenager, I began to question if God exists. This I knew: Superman was faster than a speeding bullet, more powerful than a locomotive, able to leap tall buildings in a single bound! Superman! My hero!

God took a backseat to Superman.

Interest in God came in spurts, mostly on Sundays. As a child, I loved hearing stories from the Old Testament. Those stories were as exciting as Superman's adventures.

Teetering on the brink of discovery, this simple prayer left my young adult lips: "God, if you are real, show Yourself to me."

If God really exists, does He play an active role in our lives?

Several days later…

My eye caught a disheveled elderly man on foot, wandering down the middle of the street. Is this man injured? Lost? What's wrong? I slam on the brakes and leap from the vehicle.

"Sir, are you okay?"

He mumbled something in Spanish.

Great, I neither speak nor understand Spanish! Now what? It would be wrong to abandon the old guy. Maybe thirty seconds pass, when an angel arrives. This statuesque gentleman sporting a western blazer steps out of his vehicle and walks toward us.

"What's going on?" the gentleman asks.

"This man was drifting down the street. Don't know if he's hurt or lost. I have no idea what's wrong, he speaks Spanish, and I don't."

Out of his front lapel pocket the man flashes a sheriff's badge then speaks fluent Spanish to the old guy. I know, right? Hand gestures draw attention to the matter creating the ruckus.

The sheriff smiles, turns and says, "He misplaced his belt buckle. He thought he might have lost it in the street."

"Good grief. What a relief! Glad he's not hurt. Where does he live?"

"The nursing home up the street. I'll take care of him," the sheriff reassures me.

On that note of resolution, I return to my vehicle and begin to drive away when I hear the Spirit say, *"See, I watch over my kids."*

Slap me dumbstruck!

Running on Empty

Yes, eighteen seems really young to marry. But we were in love. When we met, I was fifteen. Winchell's Donuts was my first job. He was twenty-five, divorced twice, with three kids.

What's the big deal?

Overprotective Daddy never allowed for such nonsense as dating. Who knows where that could lead?

So, out the bedroom window I'd escape to meet the irresistible man with curly, dark hair and a motorcycle. A wild start. I know.

Wedding bells rang the summer of graduation. None were pleased, but Miss Independent was of age.

It's the 1970s. Van conversions were all the rage. Ben's van was a gas guzzlin' chick magnet with a fancy mural on the side, a mini frig, a royal-blue velveteen bed nestled in the rear and gold-veined mirrors above. You know the type.

In our first year of marriage, my granddaddy passes. His funeral is at eleven o'clock tomorrow in Richland, Washington. Yours truly takes the wheel for an all-night excursion.

Departure: Long Beach, California.

Ben having worked all night, falls fast asleep in the rear of our posh mobile.

Nearly a thousand miles later, it's pitch-dark, smack-dab in the middle of no-man's land and hours away from Richland. The delirious driver glances at the gas gauge running on fumes.

How did this happen?

Before the days of 24/7 lifestyles, filling-stations were locked up tighter than granny's corset. Panic sets in.

"God, what are we going to do? We have no gas, it's the middle of the night, and we've got to be in Richland by morning."

As if God is unaware.

At this point, my connection with God is pretty superficial, but I can holler out a prayer. Since the gas gauge has failed to rise and obviously no angels on the road, I repeat the panicked prayer.

"LORD! HELLO! We need some gas down here. Please don't let us run out before we get to a pump."

Tired eyes and sweaty palms navigate the desolate winding route alongside the Columbia River. Nothing but water and asphalt. No radio reception. Nothing.

The needle never wavers.

A technique inherited from my authoritarian fourth-grade schoolteacher mom erupts. Pointing my finger to heaven, I demand, "Lord, don't let us run out of gas. I cannot miss Granddaddy's funeral!"

Under starry skies, tires follow the dark, narrow road riddled with potholes of anxiety, I implement the occasional finger just because.

Dawn breaks. A beacon of light shines to announce precious sought-after gas! "Hallelujah!" Overcome with relief I shout, "Thank you, Jesus! We made it!"

Stunned, elated, and early!

Never did the van spit nor sputter. NEVER.

A miracle! On the other side of anxiety, exhilaration and comfort await. Ben slept through the entire worrisome event. Of course, he was highly skeptical when told how far our gas guzzler traveled on fumes. You might be too.

Believe the story or not, this sole eyewitness knows what happened that miraculous night.

Bizarre as it sounds, the children of Israel wandered in the desert forty years, and their clothes never wore out. If God makes clothing last forty years, can't he make a single gallon of gas stretch hundreds of miles? Or was there any gas at all?

It's not up to me to figure it out. I just know the miraculous outcome.

This event fueled my journey to trust God. The dynamics of our relationship changed that day. Then along came a test. Test and I are not friends. Let me introduce my neighbor Mike.

Talk to Me God, Before I Slap Somebody!

Weird Mike

Mike was an odd kind of guy.
Lived by himself after his mom died.
Always thought he was kind of lazy,
And half crazy.

I can see him now,
Sittin' on the porch,
Strummin' his guitar and singin' of sorts.
Singin' so loud;
Singin' so clear
In hopes someone would hear.

You see, he had no friends,
For he was kind of weird.

Thought he was a dropout,
Then to find out
He had a college degree
In anthropology.

He must have been very smart, you see,
But what happened
remains a mystery.

Thinking back, recalling the day
The Holy Spirit spoke to me,

"Invite him over, be a friend,
He needs help you see."
"Yes, you're right, Lord,
Dinner it will be!"

Now driving down the street one day,
A familiar face coming my way.
"Hey Mike, you need a ride,
for it's oh so cold outside?"
"Only if it's not too much trouble,"
Mike replied.

Up the drive we went,
And before he departed our eyes met.
Eyes filled with despair,
So sad as if to say,
"Help me please, help me today."

Now remember, I was in a hurry,
So off to my appointment did I scurry.

I'll never forget those gazing eyes,
With their hollowness inside.
Emptiness was everywhere,
As if his only hope was a prayer.

Impressions of the soul,
How they last.
I wish dinner had come to pass.

Opportunities come and go.
For Mike and me, it will never be.

For you see,
Three days later
He entered eternity.

Divine Disguised

Two years after getting married, fresh out of college, I was penniless. Pity was had by Denver's upscale department store Neusteter's. The broke hairstylist was baptized in hoity-toity.

Euphoric utopia surrounds the rusty stylist as divas entrust me with mixing colors or blow-drying their client's hair just shy of the finishing touch.

Juggling superstars requires finesse.

Bottom of the food chain is where you'll find me. Lady Laundress and all things grunt, at your service. Hardly a glamourous position for a cosmetologist. But it's a job.

The tall handsome son hired me to assist the divas for his daddy's high-class salon. Hardly socially redeemable.

"When all the daily chores are done, you are free to go. The pay remains the same no matter the hours on the clock."

Woohoo! A meager bonus for Lady Laundress. Now, don't think I'm ungrateful. The son doesn't hold a knife to my throat or anything.

Mr. M is past his prime, no longer a fixture in his own salon. However, when he does return, noses rise with the tide. Waters part. Divas bow. Mr. M makes a splash, snaps his fingers, twirls his shears, and waves his magic brush. His audience swoons. It's quite the show.

Really, he's a bossy sort in need of a tailor, as his clothes burst at the seams. He thinks he's something of an item. I'm young, what do I know? Gotta run! I hear my name.

"Reneé, clean these mirrors!" snaps the king.

All the mirrors were just cleaned. Sure, I can do it again and again, AND AGAIN.

Gotta run! His highness calls.

"Reneé, these magazines are a mess!"

Nothing I do satisfies. UGH! All three disheveled magazines are now perfectly aligned by the king's ticked off assistant. Slave master insists all tasks be done again. That's right, AGAIN!!

Ready to snap. Mr. M can stuff his fluffy wand!

I suck it up. A pain in my royal heinie he is.

Five-thirty stares me down. Floors spit shined, waxed with my own saliva. Towels folded in ways unknown, sealed with words untold. Shampoo bowls sparkle as reflective automotive paint.

Kiss my sweet lips! Mr. M deemed Lady Laundress worthy of freedom. Steaming, I head to the parking garage.

I can't even see straight. Where on God's green earth is my hotrod? It can't be lost. It's a white '72 Cougar, like "Starsky and Hutch's" hotrod. You know, it has a cool thick red stripe over the top and sides?

There she is!

Dreamy leather bucket seats cradle and comfort one cranky soul. Ransom is paid at the booth. Smoldering, I'm ready to blast my way out of the garage when the beast drifts to a complete stop obstructing the city sidewalk. My prized possession gone lame.

No one can pass the heap blocking the exit and walkway.

Thank God! Brawny young bucks come to the rescue, pushing fat tires out of harm's way.

Gridlock was avoided by Mr. M keeping me past rush hour.

Slap me astonished!

Coveted Jacket

Capitalism is not for the weak of heart. It requires ingenuity, grit, patience, and perseverance. Money helps but is not required. Defeat frequents the door of a creative genius. The hope is that great ideas will collide with success.

Mom birthed a self-starter, an entrepreneur in child number three. Then boldly taught the risk-taker the skill of sewing. Average was not in the family vocabulary. Meticulous was. What can I say?

The Singer sewing machine smokes like a train. Excited to bring my creative ideas to life. Masterfully I stitch the frayed exterior seams on indigo denim jackets. Ordinary seams won't do. Color and texture cohesively layer each piece of wearable art.

Not sure how several discriminating buyers found their way into my living room admiring my recent creations but spend, spend, spend! One lady carefully lays three remaining jackets over her arm, fumbles through her handbag, and politely states, "I failed to bring my checkbook. Would you be so kind to allow me to mail a check?"

"Of course," I oblige.

The idea to hold the pieces until she returned, never crossed the mind of the naïve creator. I kissed three jackets and three hundred dollars goodbye. Stolen under my nose. With permission. Somebody should slap her! Or ME!

Oh, the flattering fit of a bolero. A cropped, frayed hemline nicely accentuates any slim waistline. Avoid symmetry and never duplicate the look. This is a keeper! With smug pleasure, I cautiously guard my last creation.

My bolero and I are minding our own business at the grocery store when a woman pushes her cart towards me. Eyes of adoration gaze upon the spectacular piece. "My, what a beautiful jacket you have!"

The designer pivots to give the admirer a full view. "Thank you, so much!"

"Where did you ever find such a lovely garment?"

With slight arrogance I said, "I made it."

"It's really nice," she affirms my good taste.

Confidently the snob proceeds to the next aisle. Once again, confronted with her envious eyes.

The quiet voice inside says, *"Give her the jacket."*

Give her the jacket!? I've already donated three, this is my last one. It probably wouldn't fit her anyway, I justify.

In quick pursuit of the next aisle, I fight off the voice in defense of the coveted jacket in hopes both the voice and woman disappear. NO! There she is again, the one who threatens the very existence of my last beloved creation.

Calmly the request is repeated. *"Give her the jacket."*

Covetous eyes meet resistance.

This is my *coat. I love it. She can't have it!*

Groceries in hand, pleased to have arrived home intact. *Whew! That was close! I narrowly escaped losing another jacket to a lusting woman.*

Safely I tuck the coveted piece into the hall closet. "Truly, this is one of my finer pieces," gloating over the save.

Several days pass. Fashionista needs just the right garment to finish the ensemble. I reach into the closet to retrieve the beloved bolero when I hear the words, *"You should have given it to the lady in the grocery store."*

I slam the door! Every time the closet door opens, joy is gone. The alluring creation has lost all appeal. The joy of wearing the art piece is replaced by a sore spot of my disobedience.

Never did I wear the masterpiece again. It was donated to the Goodwill.

Note to self: Just do what the Lord tells you. To have your way is not worth the disappointment. Also hold the merchandise until it's paid for.

Dog Gone It

Strange as it sounds, a puppy prepared us for children. A cute cuddly Doberman Pinscher held the position of firstborn.

Yes, the rambunctious Duke was a challenge. Establishing rules is necessary. Is the newest family member allowed on the brand-new sofa? In bed? To lick us? Eat table scraps? The list goes on and on and on. We rarely agreed. Since opposing views weren't allowed since childhood, I sucked it up and complied.

Ben enjoys watching Duke fling that old boot.

"It must hurt!"

When Duke was little, his behavior was so cute. A year later, that same behavior is no longer adorable. It's expensive. Intolerable.

One boot turned into a closet of shoes. My shoes. As in my favorite shoes.

How does one explain soiled underwear scattered about when an unexpected guest stops by? This might be normal for some households. Grumpy fails to see the humor. Now if you're looking for amusement, dress the big guy up. That's right. Now, that's a sight to behold. Every short-haired dog needs galoshes to accent his raincoat.

A dog's job is to entertain and protect. So far, Duke is best suited as entertainer. Cute and cuddly grew bigger and bigger until a dog the size of a pony shared our bed. Ugh. What's wrong with that picture?

It's not that I don't like furry creatures. It's the lack of training, destroying everything in sight, that's my issue. Dogs need to be trained! Or is it the spouse? Grumpy is the only one who thinks this behavior is *not* okay. And the incessant barking!

"Hush!" we bark back.

Duke tries to warn us, but nobody listens.

Who likes jumping dogs? Can you say, snags? Or ruined? None can deny, puppies have a knack for both. Duke's not-so-favorite human gets the honor of wearing ruined clothes.

Don't slap me down now!

Is there a parent alive who hasn't gone overboard for their child's first birthday? It's cause for a glorious cake. Child's Bakery, the most fabulous bakery ever, delivers impressive confections!

I salivate as I unbox the precious Big Bird cake and push it to the back of the countertop for safe keeping. Or so I thought.

Does the dog's guilty posture give it away? Or blue food coloring all over the teeth? Or is it the missing chunk of cake?

Mama is MAD!

Awe, the life of a spoiled dog. The tales keep coming. Some call it cute. The bell has rung. Horse races abound, sliding into tight spaces where dogs don't belong, behind the sofa, tangled up in the cord of my all-time favorite lamp.

N-O-O-O!! In slow motion, I attempt to save the golden milk jug lamp as it tumbles off the end table. My prized lamp lies in shambles. Ugh. The beautiful compliment to the sofa and accent chair now is shattered to pieces by a crazed dog.

The destruction sends this innovative designer over the sofa's edge, ready to wring Duke's neck or take the naughty dog to the pound.

When I hear, *"You wouldn't do that to your children would you?"*

Well… *Maybe I would. Which child are you referring to, Lord?*

Ben sort of forgot he had two sons. After being hounded by his young wife, two young humans appeared on our doorstep.

Lucky boys. They get their own bed.

In those days, there were no books on how to stepparent preteens. You don't know what you don't know. This I know: kids need love. A father image has been MIA for years.

Intrigued by deafening silence, I pass by Junior's bedroom. Plastered against the wall, eye to eye, Junior is held captive by fully exposed canine teeth. Duke means business.

"Duke! Get down!" I yell. "Junior, I've told you to stop tormenting him!" I scold.

Days later, in the early evening, Ben and I are sound asleep, as we work the graveyard shift. The one who sleeps through earthquakes is suddenly awakened. A rare occurrence. Maybe Duke is restless and disturbs me. I don't know.

The house smells odd. A smoky aroma. My sniffer is on high alert and discovers the source. A slight flame smolders in Junior's mattress. The pyromaniac is nowhere in sight.

Without a doubt, God protected us from his shenanigans that night. He earned the family's first nickname: Jailbird. Well deserved, Junior. Well deserved. And I thought Duke was mischievous!

Duke remained a vital part of our family until he slipped away without any assistance from the one he annoyed most.

Junior's future was sketchy. Choices. We all make them.

Shazam!

It's Tuesday morning before Thanksgiving. I should be twisting hair but NO, sleep deprived behind the court lectern, I stand.

"Turn the other cheek" the good book says. Those words are easy to quote, but when tempers flare, I can tell you, it's not easy to practice. If even possible. Last night it wasn't. This law-abiding Sunday school teacher has never been in such a pickle.

SHAZAM! How quickly life changes. Not in my wildest dreams! How did our marriage become so adversarial?

Last night was the most horrific night. Jail is not the place for a nice girl like me.

"Your Honor, why is what Ben did okay and what I did not?"

A long pause as the judge scans a host of notes before simply replying, "He defended himself."

Good Lord! Defended himself? Fumes spew from enraged nostrils. "It was a set up, I tell you! A set up!"

Ben is equally as guilty. That slammer had room for two! Although one may not have lived.

Life wasn't always in an upheaval. Sure, we had some tough times, but we also had some exceptional years. Like, when…

Chuck's Donuts

Ben lost his job. The newspaper's business section became Ben's new best friend. Life was never the same after stumbling upon this ad:

"Family-Owned Donut Shop for Sale Near Washington Park"

"Ben, have you called on the donut shop yet?" I ask.

"No, not yet, but I'm really excited."

"What are you waiting for?"

Finally! An appointment to see the donut shop. Jump in, let's go! Bask in the ambience of Wash Park, as the locals call it. Envious eyes gawk. Massive trees graciously line the shady streets. Storybook shops rub shoulders with vintage bungalows and quaint restaurants. A lake, joggers, rollerblades, bicycles, baby carriages, dogs, and all things outdoors energize the scenic park. Nothing like this is found in our hood. I'm sucked in.

We turn down Kentucky Street. "There it is!" Conjoined to other businesses, smack-dab on center stage, a nostalgic 1930s neon sign glows: CHUCK'S DONUTS.

Notice the hand scribbled "Closed for two weeks" cardboard sign propped in the corner? Busting to see the golden goose. Oh, here's our guy. "Hello Mr. B."

"Welcome." Mr. B inserts the key. The shop bells jingle. "Let's go in."

Instantly we're transported in time, tickled by a blast from the past, greeted by aged, speckled tile floors and a split dining counter.

The smitten one gently rubs the shiny chrome rib-edged laminate bar. Under the bar peeks a dozen avocado stools with matching chrome bands. "Look they swirl!"

Everything screams vintage. Everything.

"Do you like the wall separating the eating space?" I quiz.

Ben shakes his head. "People want to see the baker do his magic; it's a poor layout."

Ben nods and points out the flour dust clinging to paneled walls.

"The stainless fryer and hood are in really good shape, as is the triple sink," I remark.

"Yes, so is the baker's table and proof box. Everything else needs replaced," Ben says.

He's right. Not that there is anything wrong with a wood table held together with dollops of glaze. Ben is familiar with food handling laws from managing several different restaurants.

Ben leans in and whispers, "I've dreamed of owning a donut shop." Now, that's a news flash!

The life and times of a simply elegant 1930s bronze cash register flash before my eyes. Oh, the stories this ornate piece could tell. Unable to keep my hands off, I fondle the beautiful raised bronze design. The smitten one asks, "Does this stay?" Aged white and black keys hold me captive. Ambience sings as I push the dollar key. The drawer springs open. Intrigued, my fingers rub over the worn wooden compartments.

It takes my breath away. Above the drawer rests a marble ledge with aged glue smeared in the crack. Two crowned brass screw heads hold it all in place.

Mr. B senses my infatuation. "Everything goes with the shop," he comments.

"Something is missing." The captivated one scans for a display case. "That must be it!" I say, pointing to the slanted counter leaning against the window.

Ben announces, "We've seen enough. I'd like to examine the profit-and-loss statements."

"Of course, I'll get those to you," Mr. B replies.

Business is business; my infatuation is totally irrelevant. Account receivables are evaluated. Based on the shop's annual sales, this is a hobby. Ben makes a reduced offer on the overpriced donut shop.

Judging by Chuck's testy response, he lives in a world of delusion. "I'd rather die or see it turned into a roller rink than sell it at that price!"

Indulge the Sunday school teacher for a moment. Proverbs 18:21 says, "Death and life are in the power of the tongue." Like the law of gravity, the principle applies whether you believe in the law or not. Words are powerful.

We all fantasize over the escalated value of our possessions. Here's the problem: your sentiment has no monetary value. It's a tough reality.

Nevertheless, I love this shop! A week goes by.

"Ben, we should increase our offer."

Deflated over Ben's obstinate, "It's not worth any more." To allow an opportunity to slip through our fingertips over a few thousand dollars befuddles me! One week drags into two. I'm ready to explode.

"I'm telling you; we need to call and now is the time," I plead.

Reluctantly, Ben succumbs.

"Mr. B, we'd like to further discuss our offer on the Donut Shop."

"I'll talk to Chuck and get back to you," Mr. B replies.

Several hours pass. The phone rings.

"Sorry, they can't talk right now. The family is planning Chuck's funeral."

Mercy! Chuck's careless words left an indelible mark on this girl. Why give reason for gossipers? The increased offer is accepted.

My hairstyling career is placed on hold. Now I'm Ben's beautiful baker assistant. Impressive, I know.

Destiny calls. To fry and glaze delicate delights is my new lot in life. Ben solicits three hospitals for daily deliveries. Doors fly open. Sales explode! Our reputation grows exponentially.

Bursting with creative marketing ideas doesn't hurt either. Within hours of planting a bus bench smack-dab in front of Winchell's on South Broadway, our bench lands a prime spot in the *Rocky Mountain News*. The power of print splattered all over town!

Winchell's on South Broadway in Denver, 1981

Sales skyrocket! Evidently, the direct approach struck a chord with people hankering for extraordinary donuts. The donut snob vaguely recalls the newspaper caption, something like brilliant strategy. The bench serves both those in need of a seat and an alternative.

"Truly one of my best marketing ideas," says the donut snob turned marketer.

It wasn't long before the community stole our hearts. Customers rallied behind our T-shirt logo contest. Clever was the winning design featuring a donut-style spaceship, shooting through a galaxy of stars and planets, boasting: Chuck's Donuts Are Out of This World.

A sea of walking billboards attended our first and only donut-eating contest. Donut bribery is a delicious incentive for news media coverage.

Go ahead, call it pride, it's true. We certainly took pride in our heavenly sweet treats, but how a contestant can devour nearly one hundred donuts escapes me.

Wonder if the donut eating champion ever recovered? Light and fluffy, heavenly, or not, Alka-Seltzer had a new best friend.

After work, Ben sits at the counter with customers sharing how good God is. I recall a customer, larger than life, threw open the shop door, lifted his hands, and shouted, "You must be on drugs. No one is always this happy!"

How does one respond to that? Laughter of course! It's true. Not the drug part but being so happy. Laughter abounds. We can't help ourselves. There's nothing wrong with being your own entertainment.

Excitement brews for Christmas of '82 hosting a Christmas Eve open house right here at the donut shop. Darn that blizzard. No one in their right mind is on the streets. Daddy braves the storm to drag food and supplies for the party through two feet of snow. Like a Hallmark movie, customers either ski or snowshoe over for a memorable dose of merriment, food, love, and laughter. Community exudes.

In the middle of the night, Ben abruptly stops rolling dough. Glassy eyes turn. "I just had a vision," he says. "I was preaching in a stadium packed full of people. God told me to *'stop smoking'* so He could use me per the vision."

Ben was a natural, compelled to share. After all, it's not every day you're delivered from burdens carried, cleansed and granted a brand-new life. To be honored with a vision of destiny was beyond amazing. It was confirmation. "Did it have to come with conditions?" Ben moaned. Smoking since boyhood is tough to give up. It might sound easy, until it's not.

God does not force us to do anything.

Joy filled our busy lives the entire four years we owned the blast from the past. Ben never tried to stop smoking. Pure speculation on my part, but maybe the vision was too intimidating.

Donut sales continued to soar.

"If business was so grand, why did you sell?" you ask.

Pregnancy. Children are too precious to ignore. Long days, six days a week is not an environment to raise children in.

Customers regularly reinforced, "Children will change your life."

This twenty-eight-year-old, soon-to-be-mom didn't wait ten years for someone else to raise her child.

The cherished donut shop was listed for sale well below market value. Of course, it sells right away for the same price Chuck asked years earlier. The new owners share their idea of expanding the lunch menu.

"Eggrolls, huh? No doubt their donuts will have a unique flavor."

Panic

A built to intimidate, hostile letter lands in our mailbox shortly after selling the donut gem. The letter implies his clients paid too much for the shop and insists we buy it back. Details include their inability to incorporate the menu changes due to health department regulations.

The letter concludes, "You have two weeks to respond."

Ticked and rattled, I begin to pray, "Lord, give me strength and wisdom so I don't inadvertently choke somebody!"

An entrepreneurial spirit carries one a long way, possibly into the land of stupidity, which remains to be seen. No consideration is given to contact an attorney and no discussion is had between the two of us.

The following Sunday, a guest speaker rears off topic while teaching Sunday school and says, "This is not in my notes, I don't know why

I'm saying this, *but God is not pressured or manipulated by dates and deadlines. His deliverance is on its way.*"

My friend, did you just hear what I heard? Did that speak to you as it did me?

God heard my cry, but now what?

During the night I was awakened with an epiphany. With pen in hand the solution flowed through bony fingertips:

Dear Mr. Attorney,

We sold a donut shop, not an eggroll stand. Chuck's Donuts offered a limited lunch menu. It's incumbent upon the buyers to do their due diligence regarding Denver's food preparation regulations. They spoke of searching five years to locate an affordable donut shop. Certainly, they researched the state health regulations during that time.

Since they felt the shop was overpriced, have the business appraised and subtract our lunch sales. If the value is not worth what they paid, we will gladly refund the difference.

Sincerely,
Ben and Reneé

We never heard another word.

This event was a turning point. It taught me the importance of standing up for myself.

You ask, "Why didn't Ben tend to this situation?"

That's a really good question.

Adrenaline

Ben's sick mama passed away this past week. It's a long drive to Great Falls, Montana. The old Lincoln Continental is loaded and ready to roll. Straight through the night we'll drive with our baby girl snuggled fast asleep behind the driver's seat footwell. Mama is stretched out on the luxurious backseat.

An hour outside our destination, under the darkness of night, I'm awakened by screeching brakes, an intense swerve, and the distinct sound of glass being crushed. Mama's body thrusts forward. I brace against the driver's seat back so as not to crush our sleeping infant.

The Lincoln screeches to a stop.

Ben lunges from the vehicle. I spring upright and rub my sleepy eyes, unable to see clearly through the smoke. Smack-dab in front of the Lincoln's unscathed hood, lies a tipped over semi-trailer.

Scared eyes glare from the rear sprung gate. Cows too traumatized to scatter from the overturned trailer.

Ben shouts, "Reneé, run get help. We need an ambulance."

Where does one run in the middle of nowhere? Off in the distance shines a light, a farmhouse way across the field, maybe a mile away. Adrenaline kicks in. Haunting moos propel. Feet flee. The family sprint I never acquired emerges.

BAM! BAM! BAM! Vigorously I bang on the front door. No one answers. Who could blame them. It's the middle of the night. *Is anyone even home?* Frantically I shout, "HELP!! WE NEED AN AMBULANCE!!" No lights come on. The closed curtains never move. Not a soul in sight. Feverishly these legs sprint back to the accident.

By the time I return, the air has cleared. Crumpled up in the middle of the road is an old rusty green pick-up cradling a badly injured man slumped over in the front seat. It reeks of booze and vomit.

Ben takes his pulse.

"Does he need mouth to mouth?"

"No, he's breathing, but barely. Did you get an ambulance?"

"Who knows. We can hope." Simultaneously I catch a glimpse of the rattled semi-truck driver wandering about.

Fortunately, a state trooper arrives, looks inside the truck cab, and comments, "We knew this day was comin'. Just a matter of time. Ol' Bill was always drinkin' 'n' drivin'."

I have a notion to slap that trooper. If I hadn't experienced the devastation firsthand, I might have felt different.

Our efforts to get medical attention fail to snatch Bill from death's grip.

A trip laden with grief. Ben's mom lies in state adjacent to Bill's room. Strange. Hard to overcome the sense we narrowly missed our own appointment with death.

How close was it? I have no idea. The scared one knows this: God protected us.

How *do* you stop someone from driving drunk?

Clothing a Legend

YOU might ask, "Why did a suburban couple get involved with an inner-city church?"

God was there. It was fresh. The sanctuary was packed with all flavors and colors, poor and wealthy, old and young, misfits and addicts. Like nothing we'd ever experienced. People hungry for God.

Seems God takes pleasure in shaking up religious notions by doing the unexpected. New Life Church conformed to no man's mold, starting with the pastor. Hear tell, no one else wanted the motley crew. The clock held no restrictions to the Sunday afternoon services. Gifts of the Spirit flowed.

We grew. We flowed. We loved. We stretched.

Confirmation over and over to our call flowed, including Ben's call to preach the gospel worldwide. The Lord's simple request of Ben to quit his thirty-year habit of smoking must have been weighty. He dug in his heels.

Fearful? Maybe.

It was common for Charlotte to preach barefoot on stage. This precious woman was authentically real, not stuffy. She delivered and brought even the most pretentious of audiences to their knees or had them in stitches. Joy and love oozed from her pores. Char's fluffy size could not begin to hold her enormous heart. God broke the mold after creating this beautiful woman.

Hardly ordinary. Human nonetheless.

Rarely do we witness such compassion or anointing. She taught fresh revelation to parishioners. A favorite topic covered by Charlotte was our flesh nature contending with our spirit man. It's a tough one. Simply put, our flesh nature derives great pleasure from doing what it wants. Do I need a list? You know the dirty pleasures: gossiping or slapping people or holding an offense.

The list is endless. Sorry if I missed yours.

"Honey, would you sew for me?" Charlotte asked. Now, when admirers of my sewing skills approach, it's a compliment but also a double-edged sword.

I hesitated as my flesh takes NO pleasure in sewing for others.

"What do you have in mind?"

"Can you copy this dress? I'd like another just like it. I'd sure appreciate it, honey."

Big Charlotte was such a giver, known to give the shoes off her feet and her last dollar to those in need. How could I say no? That was the beginning of a long relationship with the finest woman I've ever known. Charlotte Cronk was my pastor. I was her seamstress, and occasionally her hairdresser, but always her friend.

One dress turned into countless others. For years I kept the woman of God in our version of haute couture. It didn't matter what was dreamed up. Charlotte always squealed with pleasure at the outcome. Design, pattern, and fabric selection were my pleasure. Ingredients for joy were as simple as hot pink and steel gray.

Anything glittery always spun her head and looked great against her shiny silver hair. Char loved ruffles, rarely the choice of most women her size.

Handmade sparkly creations frequently graced her shoulder. If Char didn't give away the accessories, someone would lift them. Everyone wanted a piece of Charlotte. I'd whip up replacements for missing parts 'n' pieces.

People clamored to her side in hopes of receiving a *word* as she operated liberally in the prophetic. It didn't matter where Charlotte was, impartation flowed. No one was beneath her. Selflessly, Charlotte poured love into the lives of the poverty stricken and presidents of nations. Charlotte relayed the story of sitting next to Nelson Mandela discussing destiny. People around the world were touched by this vessel of love and the anointing she carried. Wherever Char was, love was certain to flow.

"Honey, God loves you and I do too," with a warm smile she'd say. Irresistible! What do you do but flow with it?!

Pokes are commonplace for those who play with pins and needles. When stitching my own clothing, spouts of blood oozed on occasion. Not so, when sewing on Charlotte's wardrobe. No matter the severity of the jab, blood never flowed. Never. Not even when squeezed.

No garment of Charlotte's ever left my sewing table without being saturated in prayer. A prayer for healing to those who touch her garment, just as the lady in Matthew 9:21 said, "If I could but touch the hem of his garment, I'll be healed." I believe the same for Charlotte. For signs and wonders to follow this precious sister.

Revelation of the *living word* oozed from her being.

Our relationship flowed in much the same anointing. The Spirit would reveal a need, and I'd go to praying.

Charlotte told me, "I can feel your prayers."

Her comment humbled and stunned me.

One night I dreamed of a beautiful black-and-white tailored dress. Not the typical circular ruffle dress Charlotte wore. The dream dress featured an offset row of tiny white pleated chiffon ruffles. Thanks to fishing line, twirly ends ruffle. Gradually the ruffles enlarged, cascading into a twelve-inch swirly hemline. It was so Charlotte! This seamstress was compelled to create the exquisite dress! So, I did. Charlotte wore it until it was threadbare.

Our inner-city church loved to participate in Denver's annual Saint Patrick's Day parade. Visions dance in my head. What Big Charlotte needs is a clown suit! Brainstormed an oversized red-and white-striped suit with polka-dots on top joined by an expansive center hoop. Not certain it was quite right, but close. I held out for perfection.

It didn't take long. *HEARTS!* Not polka-dots. Hearts are what she needs. The minute Charlotte laid eyes on the suit, she gleefully screamed, "I was thinking hearts!"

Charlotte paraded all over South Africa in the silly suit, delivering love, food, candy, and joy to children who possessed absolutely nothing.

"The people in South Africa had never seen a clown suit," said the thrilled one.

Char's clown suit in front of my home

Africa stole her heart. Char left the States to follow her dream.

Big Charlotte transitioned into *Big Mama,* describing whom she had become to people she loved more than life itself. Big Mama poured the love of Jesus into her beloved Africans.

Talk to Me God, Before I Slap Somebody!

Married Single

Connecting dots was a slow go. Awareness suddenly came upon me. My spouse and I did absolutely nothing together. Nothing. Ben no longer attends church, neither did we have meaningful discussions. Reality slapped me in the face. I am a married single.

Life's treacherous water is difficult to navigate. A delicate dance. Joy teeters with misery. My parents were poor role models in the marriage department. The two never addressed matters of importance, not in front of the kids anyway. No wonder my marriage looked the same. I didn't know any different. Undealt with issues evaporate, right?

Married singles. Undeniably flawed. Even though Ben had three stabs at marriage, neither of us figured out what it took to build a healthy relationship. How does one polish a marriage to keep it shiny? Or resurrect it from the ash heap?

Failed marriages don't just happen. They unexpectedly creep up.

Maybe that's what pushed me into God's presence. The need to connect. Feel loved. Be heard. Validation.

Life is hardly one dimensional. It's a kaleidoscope of intriguing colors and nuances. Embrace the intrigue. Go for the gusto, says the married single. You can do this girl!

Now, don't go feeling sorry for me. Life is complicated. We all have issues. I frequently tell my Bible class, "You must need this really bad for me to have the experience."

Angelic Visitation

Mundane hides tender. Bedtime for example. Classic moments pop up when least expected.

Shortly after being tucked into bed, four-year-old Sunshine a.k.a. Little Bird, makes her way into our bedroom and tugs on the covers for attention.

"Mom, I'm scared."

"You'll be fine," rolls off the tongue to shoo her away. On second thought, I pull her close. "Let me pray for you. Father, place your angels around precious Sunshine. Keep her safe while she sleeps. In Jesus' name, amen."

Sunshine shuffles back to bed in her pink onesie. All is quiet. ZZZ's fly. Unexpectedly, pitter-patter of little feet once again deliver floppy brunette curls to mom's bedside.

"Mommy, I'm scared. There's an angel in my room!"

"Go back to bed, Sunshine."

"I'm scared."

Mom snaps, "The angel won't hurt you."

She returns to her bedroom. The angel disappears from sight, but never from memory.

Years later when asked specifically about the angelic appearance, Sunshine said, "It was neither male nor female. The angel shined so brightly, almost blinding, as it guarded my bedroom."

Rich Man, Poor Man

White sandy beaches, adventures galore carried on tropical breezes in a land far far away. In a land where dreams are made for landlocked people like me, the island of Cozumel, Mexico. What a thrill!

We don't get out much.

Number one priority, is to learn to dive. Stan and Connie are nearly pro divers. I rarely dived into the pool's deep end as a child as it was way too scary.

We practice adulting now.

Dive master Himey meets us at the hotel pool to teach us how to breathe underwater. A test run of sorts. It doesn't take long; fear and heart issues eliminate Ben from sea diving. But I can go!

Ah, beach life, bask in the tranquility. Like mountain life, only different.

"There's a sunken plane off Cozumel's coast. That's where we'll be diving. It was part of a movie," Himey tells me and the guy joining us.

"That's what they say," the comrade says, doubting the story's legitimacy. He's only here for his dive certification, not a Fantasy Island tale.

Crystal-clear waters, uncluttered sandy white beaches hold an allure for this mountain gal.

Filled with excitement and apprehension, we gear up—wet suit, tank, regulator, mask, and fins—and begin the awkward walk backward toward pristine water.

"Senora *Reneé*, you look lovely in Lycra," Himey says, admiring the view before reaching the cool waters. Offended ladies might slap the poor guy. Himey is harmless. Who doesn't appreciate being admired? Winky, winky.

Ben hangs back at the seawall to observe.

Into the cool blue abyss the nervous one holds her breath and follows the fearless leader backwards into the water.

Her heart races. Hyperventilation screams.

Breathe Reneé, don't panic. Just breathe.

Lift off! Fins flutter. No longer can I hold my breath.

Slow it down girl. Slow it down. Scary moments for a landlocked gal. *Relax. There's oxygen!* I settle into a groove, trusting there will be another breath.

Himey keeps watch on my regulator dial to make sure I'm not sucking air too quickly and am not in imminent danger.

Under the magical sea we descend. Not many fish in sight. Along comes an eel. I barely get a glimpse. My diving partner taps me on the shoulder and points. Himey grabs my hand and guides me in the opposite direction. Darn! I missed a good look at that eel, the only sea life to be found.

After completing our dive, we gather on the beach. Excited, my dive partner asks, "Did you see the eel?"

With an evil eye, I glance at Himey, "No, Himey spun me around, so I missed it."

"It was so cool. I'm sorry you missed it," he sympathizes.

"Me too." Irritated, inquiring minds want to know, "Himey, why did you lead me away?"

"Ben said you were afraid of anything that moves."

"REALLY?!" I AM TICKED! What does Ben need? You got that right! Why would he undermine me like that? The first and only time this babe ever went diving, spoiled!

Snorkeling the tranquil Caribbean waters more than makes up for the eel mishap. Like a kaleidoscope! Splashes of vibrant colored fish in every direction. A phenomenal underworld happening.

Later that day we wander into town to shop.

"Rich American, take us home," the shopkeeper says. "Señora, we be your gardener and housekeeper."

I shake my head. "No, I'm not rich."

"OH, YES YOU ARE," the voice of the Lord boldly responds.

My perspective changed that day. I am sooo rich! On the other hand, they too are rich. It just looks different.

Note: Letting go of Ben's demeaning behaviors just became a way of life. "Let it roll off a duck's back," *they* say. I thought that's what I did. Little did I know, instead, those digs were buried deeper and deeper, covered under heaps of denial.

Exposed

Jailbird has flown the coop. Remember the pyromaniac? His younger brother, Dirty Bird, has come home to roost on a more permanent basis. Age never prohibits family birdlets from nesting under our roof. Meals, laundry, showers are more than adequate for our aged-out fluffy ones.

As the years passed, we'd tease Dirty Bird: "When you turn thirty, we're flying the coop, leaving no forwarding address."

Dirty Bird had other plans.

Ben, a.k.a. Big Bird, tweets out some unexpected news: "Dirty Bird moved out!" Good Lord! Why didn't he say good-bye? This seemed calculated and cruel but not surprising as Dirty Bird hasn't spoken to me in months.

Sure-fire way to hurt me to the core is the silent treatment.

Mama Bird's philosophy is honest, frank, and direct. In my dyslexic world, it avoids barriers. None of this subliminal "beat around the bush" nonsense. Such qualities have fallen out of favor in a sugar-coated society. It just ain't right.

Straight shooters hold a great appreciation for not second-guessing what others mean. To unscramble someone's intentions leaves room for grave misunderstandings. I don't get it.

Birdlets have no tastebuds for frank, open, and direct. Tweet. Tweet.

Thirty days later, another tweet ruffles Mama's feathers. Dirty Bird wants to fly back to roost.

"No way! Not until we talk." Mama Bird is angry.

My mission: To discover the root cause of Dirty Bird's prevailing silence.

Early birds flock to the kitchen a few days later to discuss the messy details. The conversation lingers as if yesterday.

Silence permeates the kitchen, a.k.a. the courtroom. Anticipation of Mama Bird's dreaded appearance to officiate causes Dirty Bird to sweat. The mid-twenty-year-old defendant fidgets at the breakfast bar.

Big Bird cowardly tucks into the adjacent room to watch fireworks from a distance. Morning sunrays spotlight Dirty Bird's blond hair. He knows he's in the birdcage.

Oxygen is sucked out of the room as the awkward silence is broken by Mama Bird's opening statement: "I asked the Lord why you won't talk to me. He says, *'you're offended by me.'*"

Instantaneous words flew. "DAD SAID, you'd kick me out of the house if you knew I was doing drugs."

Stunned. Hypnotized by lies.

The trial takes a nasty turn. Never underestimate an angry bird, particularly one with a propensity for violent behavior.

Appalled, the judge smacks down the accusation: "I never said or even alluded to that. I can speak for myself. I'll let you know if there's an issue."

Man in the shadows requires a divine intervention. Strangulation is on the docket.

"GUILTY of conspiring with the accomplice! NO, you can't stay here!"

Flaming darts shoot from beady eyes. Set ablaze, the angry Mama judge spews, "How dare you tell Dirty Bird I'd kick him out! We both knew he was on drugs. Was I your scapegoat?"

"Case closed!" What a debacle.

Betrayal showed its ugly head that day. Repercussions of offense laid bare, no place to hide. Horribly debilitating actions choked our marriage. Restraint in the highest form prevented pure evil from having its way that fine day.

Truly a divine intervention. For all the flock.

Anxiety

Being a stay-at-home dad has perks. You get to attend all the kid's school events, show your children how to cook, play and travel while the rest of the world goes to work.

Ms. Self-Sufficient is hardly pleased with life's recently dealt hand. "This is not the way it was meant to be!" the mad one declares.

It was part of our marriage vows. Following Ben's back injury, I carried the load, financially and otherwise.

Life detours, some are great, others highly overrated.

As a working mom, "fun" perks disappear. What happens when life dishes the unexpected? Put your big girl panties on and move forward. So, I do and am pretty good at it too.

It isn't a cakewalk, but challenge is my middle name.

Most salon owners survive three years. Not me.

The atmosphere changes whenever Ben enters the salon. He takes great pleasure in undermining me in front of clients and coworkers.

"Ignore him; it'll go away," says the fool in denial.

∞∞◡

Some people flow in works of excellence, perfection if you will. The rest of us, well, we have issues. This girl's pedigree proudly shines with anxiety. It was not taught rather caught, and I caught a fine case. When plans are interrupted, froth and frenzy set in. Anxiety naturally flows from my very core; it's who I am.

Riveting pain roamed my body. This anxious one received a diagnosis of fibromyalgia. Within days of the diagnosis, a friend hands me a book, *A More Excellent Way: Spiritual Root Causes of Sickness and Disease* by Pastor Henry Wright.

How appropriate and timely.

The hard truth stares me down, looks into my soul, and uncovers my deepest, darkest issues. Can't speak for the rest of you, but in my case, it's like the book read my private mail.

According to Henry Wright, autoimmune disease is caused by fear, stress, anxiety, and lack of feeling protected and covered.

BINGO!

Let's look at *covered* from the opposite direction. To *uncover* is to lay bare, expose, not feel protected, set up for ridicule or shame. When you love someone, you protect the one you love, you defend them. Hmm.

Stress, who me? Ms. Self-sufficient? Juggler of chaos? Ugh.

Tattling family members frequently interrupt my day to referee.

Why does a father engage in tattling behavior with his teenager?

Working mom sports her cape of fortitude to confront the source, "Ben, the book says my symptoms are caused by my not feeling protected or covered."

Ben shrugs, "I can't help how you feel." Assuming no responsibility for his humiliating actions in front of my colleagues must be an ultra-ego booster. Somebody should slap that man.

Why would a man purposely slander his wife?

Henry's book strikes straight at the heart of fibromyalgia. Ms. Self-Sufficient's feistiness is sucked out, beaten down and nowhere to be found. Too weak of heart to fight.

I cry out, "Lord, you need to cover and protect me."

This girl knows when she's smitten with anxiety.

"Lord, what is it?"

Then came a blast of revelation.

"You don't trust anyone to do what they said, including Me."

"Wow!" Never saw that coming.

"Somebody, slap that girl!"

Heavenly Father knows exactly what makes me tick.

Gulp, "Lord, help me trust You."

Battle of the Curse

Let this incident go on record as a defining moment in the heart of an anxious hairstylist. Maybe yours too.

The Lord dropped this revelation: *anxiety is a choice*.

DROP THE MIC!

Will I allow anxiety to run rampant and ruin my health or break from the curse and choose to trust?

Twelve inches of snow blankets the town. Friday before sunrise, snowflakes hurl from this working girl's cape as she removes tons of snow from the salon's sidewalk.

Frozen hands thaw. Now to wash up. As the water faucet twists, cries of desperation spout out.

"OH, NO!"

It's a simple rule, colors and perms require water.

Hyperventilation ensues.

Old habits are hard to break. Circumstances are fluid. On a good day, responses are somewhat controllable. Between exhales, words leak from panicked lips: "Lord, I choose to trust you." Again, "I choose to trust you."

Have you ever fought demons whispering in your ear? Hearing words like, *You're justified to slap somebody!?*

Hissy fits are unbecoming in grown-ups.

"Remain calm. Choose an alternative."

Instead, call the landlord.

"Lord, I choose to trust you." Call it a mantra if you wish. The struggle is real. *Self, don't take the challenge lightly. Break from tradition. Trust God no matter what you think, feel, or see. All else is irrelevant. Reneé, just do it!*

The clock strikes eight. Where is everyone? None of the stylists have called or shown up. There is no water, but they don't know that. Anxiety beats at the door, to torment.

Nearly hysterical, I resist and declare, "I choose to trust you, Lord." There's only me to slap sense into. BREATHE and STOP worrying!

Salvation has come! This is the second time building owner Bill was waylaid from his day job to tend to frozen pipes. He wrapped pipes with heat tape and declared, "This could take a while for the pipes to thaw. Hopefully they won't burst."

Anxiety screams, "SAY WHAT?! BURST?!"

Heat tape saves the day. What a great idea! Capitalism at work!

Half the day has slipped away. The salon remains quiet. Perplexed, and surprised, where is everyone?

Sound of rushing water tickles my ears. Elation erupts! We are in business! That is, should anyone appear.

Timing written for a Hollywood script couldn't be sweeter. Cold air bursts through the door. A flood of patrons and stylists. Go figure! No one knew of the salon's predicament. It was never discussed. The remainder of the day ran as smooth as a fine-oiled machine.

To choose to trust is priceless. The best lessons are not explained but lived out. I'm so grateful for this life changing experience.

Anxiety was put to rest. I declared a halt to phone calls refereeing those acting like children. Root causes are dealt with and reinforced. Ben never asked how I felt uncovered. It didn't matter. God covered me. He had to, for what was to come.

My marriage felt empty. Incomplete. I became invisible.

Offense

Yesteryear's single stall bathroom accommodations are tight in the ol' salon. Who'd have thought it necessary for the salon owner to assume guard duty? The beefy guard takes a protective stance to create privacy between the wheelchair-bound client and an intruder attempting to sneak a peek.

The nerve! Appalled by the audacity! Is there no decency? I can't believe my eyes. Despicable.

The annoyed guard snaps, "Excuse me, the restroom is occupied. Do you mind giving her some privacy?"

Ms. Rude storms off.

The more thought I give to the crude incident, the madder I become. "God, unless you tell me otherwise, I'll ask Ms. Rude not to return."

That'll slap her rude heinie! In Christian love of course.

The problem is, she is not my client. Hostility simmers. Options are weighed. To ask a client not to return could cause the loss of a stylist. The day of reckoning is upon us. God is apprised of my decision to exile the despicable woman.

The ticked salon owner hears, *"Tell her you're sorry for offending her."*

"SAY WHAT?!!! Do you know how awful she was!!?" The mere idea of an apology appalls me! An attempt to barter for a less merciful plan is expressed yet there comes no rebuttal to my argument.

The ticked owner prefers the slap method! Negotiation falls flat.

Note: In case you didn't catch it, God did not tell me to apologize.

Concession to choose obedience is made. Not because I want to mind you.

"Okay Lord, you win. Help my heart to agree with your request."

The clock strikes ten. The woman in desperate need of you know what saunters in. Sorely displeased doesn't begin to describe my attitude toward this morning's directives.

Self, suck it up! God help me.

I look straight into the woman's nasty brown eyes, muster up the nerve to kindly say, "I am sorry I offended you last week."

Don't kid yourself, my heart is not in this apology. This is sheer obedience. Acceptance is made, and I move on.

Being the sensitive type, I cry out, "Lord, help my heart to line up with the apology." The prayer bears repeating again and again as it is a battle to bite thick lips and withhold backhanded spontaneous reflexes.

Thirty minutes later, the stunned hairstylist reports, "Reneé, according to my client you are the best thing since sliced bread. I'm not sure what happened, but you have a friend for life. She's never spoken nicely of anyone all the years I've known her."

SHUT MY MOUTH!!! Knock me over with a feather.

To show random acts of kindness to offenders renders the most unexpected outcome. Lessons of the heart. How they last.

Could it be, to be offended is human?

And what about slapping? Or is that just me?

Speaking of Offense

Not to brag, but this "hairapist," has developed a listening ear without judgment. I know, right? That's not always been the case. After this story you might not agree.

A middle-aged man sits in my chair, sharing his horrific hair woes. At first, I'm sympathetic to his cause.

"Nobody in this town knows how to cut hair," he politely informs the fussy one wielding the sheers. Mister GQ begins to demonstrate the proper angle to hold the dangle and snip.

In amazement I listen, not at his technique but his audacity. I can only assume this explanation is intended for me to follow his explicit directives.

Let's just say, Mister GQ's approach is extremely demeaning. In fact, his insinuation was so offensive, I stop cutting his hair, stand directly in front of him and bluntly ask, "If your cuts are so great, why are you sitting in my chair?"

Of course, the question is met with cool silence.

"Sir, I have been cutting hair for twenty-five-years, and I'm darn good at it."

Because I'm in charge and wield sharp sheers, I press on: "How would you like it if I came into your place of business and told you how to do your job?"

Mr. GQ departed wearing an excellent cut but tongue-tied. Never to be seen again. To his credit, his tip equaled the price of his haircut. Hopefully, I left a lasting impression.

He'd have been out on his keester if the shrinking violet wasn't … you know? Reformed.

The Flame

In the setting of an old cobblestone village
I chase my Lover
Calling out to Him

Flirtatiously, He hides Himself from me
Yet I hear His voice
Beckoning me to find Him

The moon softly lights our path
Romance fills the air
I sense His presence everywhere

Now the table has turned
On the old narrow streets
We find ourselves once again

Only this time
I am not crying out for Him
He for me, desiring me, searching, calling
Wondering where I might be

I sense His presence
I hear His voice
My heart begins to rejoice
Tears fill my eyes
As my Lover calls out with a cry

"I have a flame for you
You are my Bride."

Photograph by Pat Kanan
"Doors To The Old World"
Eguisheim, France

The Flame
1st Place Winner
CCWC 2016 Poetry Award
(Colorado Christian Writers Conference)

EQUINE TIME

Sport Meets Divine

The Glow

Many little girls fantasize about owning a horse. Sunshine's head was filled with ideas by some wranglers in Cody, Wyoming. It was hopeless to fight. Our Little Bird joined the equine drill team Westernaires. Not hardly a "rich kid" sport as portrayed by those who knew nothing about the organization. Every other Saturday Sunshine and Ben horsed around with their new family at Westernaires.

Every child was assigned a horse for their hour-long ride. The one to avoid like the plague was Smokey, a nearly twenty-eight-year-old crotchety horse. After a year of riding, Sunshine draws the dreaded short straw.

With great enthusiasm, several spectators repeated this story, therefore it must be so.

Mischievous horses are equipped with a special knack to dump their riders. You'll know it's coming when a horse lowers its head, then fires off a quick rear fling. It's great fun for a horse to see a rider fly overhead. Scary for parents.

According to eyewitness accounts, ornery Smokey wildly bucked a time or two. Little Bird remained planted in the saddle, took control of the temperamental beast, and rode him like a champ! The crowd rose to their feet with a roar, applauding her brave accomplishment.

A proud mama moment, although I was not there to verify its authenticity.

My daughter, the legend.

Sunshine excelled in poise and control in the saddle. A leader in the making. She tried out for a special team and made it and was given leadership placement. Sunshine was a rising star.

Teenagers with attitude. Attitude has a glow, a presence, an air. Some glow more than others.

Now puppies are cute, and so are kittens. But the day we bought a horse, the family dynamics changed. Unlike dogs or cats, horses don't sleep in our bed. Finally, something we could agree on! Want some hair-raising, nail-biting horse adventures? Read my other book: *Cody Life Lessons Inspired by My Spirited Mare.*

Cody was a great match for Sunshine. Both glowed with attitude. Lots of attitude. Impressive to watch little girls close up 'n' personal transform into capable young ladies.

Westernaires became ingrained in our lives, so the day Sunshine announced "I quit!" was unexpected and painful.

"SAY WHAT!!?" I wanted to slap that child to the moon and back! Why would she do this? We just bought the horse. Yeah, Cody wouldn't load into the trailer, but she had before. This could be fixed. I was furious! Yes, Cody was stubborn. Yes, Cody had issues. But to so quickly give up? Who was this child?

Six weeks later, Sunshine's Mama rescued Cody from decaying away! Learning to ride revolutionized my life. Cody became my lifeline in a marriage set ablaze. A diversion. A source of joy.

Cody was instrumental as healer of my brokenness.

The Move

Painting by Joan Ames

Time to make the move
On to greener pastures
Only Cody didn't want to

Come on Cody
There's fresh grass to be had
Room to roam beats a stall
Can't be all bad

On the journey we began
Forging our way to Cody's dismay
Please don't make me beg
Cody had her own idea
Attitude it would be

Leaving friends behind
She did not embrace
Determined to set the pace
Cody voiced her view
In the middle of the road
With a mighty episode

Rearing up like Trigger and Roy
Planted in the saddle
Sure-footed and stout
"This is not a democracy
You have not a vote!"
I said with a pop and a shout

Now Cody girl
I mean you no harm
It might be scary
But, Darlin'
You'll even have a barn

On that note we did trod
When clearly I heard a
Word from God....

*"She's just like My children
Acting as if I don't know what's best.
They balk at Me too
and put Me to the test.
Not wanting to leave*

their friends behind

and

Experience something new.

The plans I have prepared

Are grand too!"

For the Love of a Horse

Self-appointed twelve-year-old instructor Savanah proudly teaches grooming to the equine newbie old enough to be her mother.

"Turn the clippers on directly in Cody's line of vision. Now Cody, don't be scared," Savanah chatters over clattering clippers caressing my mare's swan neck. "She needs to know the blades won't hurt her."

The little darlin' hands over the worn clippers and says, "You're on your own."

With a swath, black silken goatee hair flutters to the ground. That wasn't too bad, for a first timer. No cuts, nips, or attitude. I've never given a beautification treatment to a horse.

"Cody, all the other temperamental mares will envy you."

Savanah insists all furry feathers need to be clipped from the backside of her hooves.

Cody's rear end is positioned in my face. Her hoof is neatly tucked between my thighs. Buzz goes the clippers. Fluffy fetters float freely in the breeze. I step back to admire my handiwork. "You clean up real fine, girl." Resuming the position for another stroke.

As a flash of lightening across the sky, this babe catapults through the air! Yes, airborne! Twenty feet from where I stood mere seconds before. Dazed, in the dirt the limp dishrag lies.

Excruciating pain rushes to my left shin.

"Ooooo, man that hurts!"

Breathless, stunned, and limp, the dishrag gathers her heap of sore bones from the unforgiving ground and hobbles up the rickety steps into the tack room. Unscathed britches drop to the ankles. A freakin' purple balloon resides on my shin. Purple screams serious! If there's a cowgirl hall of fame, this certainly qualifies for induction.

Self, what does one do when clobbered by a horse? Option number one, seek medical attention. Option two, pray. God's been teaching me about praying over injuries. By now I've experienced a couple of them. OK, maybe more than a couple. Alright, quite a few. To date, this is the worst.

The Bible teacher emerges. Scriptures infuse this painful bag of bones. "Speak to your mountain,"[1] which happens to look like a giant purple balloon right now! In Jesus' name, I grab my shin bone and painfully declare, "If I agree touching anything it shall be done."[2] Reneé, don't pay attention to how it looks, "walk by faith, not by sight."[3] Get busy believing! Because "Nothing is impossible"[4] for those who believe.

---

1   Mark 11:24

2   Mark 16:18

3   Corinthians 5:7

4   Matthew 17:20

There is no one else here to agree with you, agree with the Word! Your very leg and livelihood depend on it!

You might ask, "Didn't you panic?" Amazing how skills rise in a time of crisis. You cannot act upon what you do not know. You'll only react. This is not the time to doubt whether the Word is true or not.

Don't stand there gawking at your bellowing bruised shin; do what you know to do, take authority as Jesus taught! Command the mountain of pain to align with healing. Get to praying, girl! You know God heals. Practice what you believe! Put those big girl panties on and do it!

Holding back tears, I grab my throbbing shin, "I command bruising, pain, swelling, and any repercussion of this injury, in the name of Jesus, be gone!" Infused with resolve, "There!" I hoist my unscathed pants up and limp back to the hitching post where Cody remains composed as if nothing happened. I refuse to allow this incident to interfere with our ride.

"Cody, let's saddle up!" It would profit nothing to slap her. Although I sure would have liked to.

While my shin throbs, I praise and thank God for healing, no matter how it felt. I refuse to come into agreement with the pain, only the healing. This I have learned well. Tenacity is good for something!

Within an hour of riding, the pain subsides.

Back at the corral, the lame cowgirl hobbles to the tack room and pulls down her britches to examine her leg. How can this be? The purple is totally gone! The massive swelling has nearly disappeared! Fingers gently massage the bone in amazement. It doesn't feel broken. Cody kicked my shin bone dead center. Wow! Only a slight scrape remains.

A MIRACLE! God is awesome! Blown away, speechless, and grateful, I hobble down the stairs.

Tenderness lingered an entire year, a subtle reminder of the miracle received. Never did I limp or miss work. This forty-year-old cowgirl-wannabe weathered that storm well.

Out of Control

Photo by Tonya Vander

I have a horse
Cody is her name
She taught me much
To her I'll blame
She likes to do her own thing

Out in the pasture we rode
Headed to the barn we did go
I did not give her the lead
Cody merely took it from me

Like a flash of lighting
We did fly
Never touching the ground
What a high!

My heart beating fast
Exhilaration I did feel
So out of control it was surreal!

Tried so hard to pull back on the reins
Only to feel the ground's rocks
Once again

What a thrill at the time
I could have been killed
That wasn't God's time or plan
For I lived to tell the story once again

A valuable lesson
For which Cody gets the blame
A mare out of control
is a VERY DANGEROUS thing!

Horses and people are much the same

No better therapist than Cody. A teacher too. An instrument of wisdom used by the Spirit of God. A reprieve from the hostile life inside four walls called home.

Miracle by Night

Horses and people are much the same. Personalities are spirited, independent, and tenacious. One could say, we have attitude. Today we are off to the arena for some serious horsin' around. Riding alone is often preferred, unless of course, a mischievous horse "dumps" the rider.

Moments like these, a rider appreciates having spectators around for the rescue. It's pure speculation how my head missed smashing into the lower corral bars. Destruction gone awry.

Cowgirl up, Reneé! Get back in the saddle. Nobody is going to feel sorry for you. Just do it! Slowly the gravel-embedded face rises from the sand. *Okay, so my neck is jarred. Cowgirl up! No whining.* Not until I grab the saddle horn, does my hip scream.

A little pain has never stopped you before. Are you going to start now? Downing doses of encouragement like shots of whiskey to sedate the aches. So, it hurts like the devil! You can do this!

Reality sets in. Cowgirl, this ride is over. Done.

I know we just got started. Gotta get home. Hopefully my friends are at the barn to pray.

Skinned hands wrap over the hurtin' hip. With a stiff upper lip, the wounded cowgirl prays, "I take authority over pain, bruising, and any repercussion. In Jesus' name."

The crippled one bobbles about unsaddling the mischievous horse. Pain intensifies. Tears flow.

Painfully, Cowgirl's booty slowly slides into the lowest seat ever made, Toyota's Corolla.

Oooooo, it's a tough ride home.

Intolerable pain is eased by youthful bubbly charm. "Come on Mom, we're going to Dirty Bird's." Sunshine's persistence bears a strong resemblance to her shelty's begging behavior.

"Now?" I whine, not letting on about the pain.

"Come on, Mom, let's go."

"Really, Sunshine? I've just driven twenty miles. To go across town again? I'm just not up to it."

"Come on, Mom."

"I smell like a horse."

"They don't care. Let's go." My fourteen-year-old excels in barking orders to the elderly and wounded.

Blind as bats, neither Sunshine nor her father notice I'm severely buggered up. Maybe they deem this slow pace as normal. They just pay me no mind.

Eyes roll as this martyr hobbles to the truck. The ease of climbing up into the truck cab is far less painful than the booty drop into my low-rider.

Ben and Sunshine scamper down Dirty Bird's hallway, leaving me to fend for myself. The newly handicapped babe had no idea apartment hallways stretch the length of a football field. Every step is more grueling than the last.

Odd, my bullet-proof prayers are totally useless.

It never occurs to me to amend my prayers with the important clause, "and no fractures or broken bones."

Agony blocks recollection of details. This I do recall, it smarts a whole lot to lie down with a possible hip fracture. A struggle between hip and desire is real. My body finally surrenders to the bed.

Desperate for serious prayer, not someday, but NOW! I slowly roll toward the bedside table, grab the phone, and dial my friends. Ugh. No response. "Leave a message after the tone."

"Stan and Connie, pray for me. Cody threw me today. My hip hurts REALLY BADLY. I can't walk, and I work in the morning. Thanks."

Lights out.

Now, you might ask, why didn't I go to the ER? This isn't my first rodeo. God always heals me. I *expect* healing. The thought of *not* getting healed isn't even on my radar.

None of this six-week recovery business. Besides, there is no time for hospitals. I work tomorrow.

The morning alarm blares. Out of bed I jump. That's right, you heard me. I jump out of bed! Stop in my tracks. This is not the same traumatized body I took to bed last night.

"Thank You, Jesus, my Deliverer, my Healer!!" Gratefulness and thanksgiving flood my soul. Off to work I go. No limp. No pain.

God is beyond awesome! Do you think God favors me? I certainly do. But I'll let you in on a secret, He favors you too!

Proverbs 8:35 (NASB) says, "For he who finds Me, finds life. And obtains favor from the Lord," See, you too can be His favorite.

He takes great pleasure in showing off. Expect it. I do.

Afterthought: Don't think for a moment my life is in a constant state of pain. It is not. I tend to be joyful, although that trait may not shine all the time, due to topic and season, there is a reason.

Epiphany

"All things are possible to those who believe" (Mark 9:23 NASB). Some adopt this as an inspirational mantra. It's my lifestyle.

A matter of survival causes one to evaluate, do miracles exist? I was taught miracles passed away with the disciples. My spirited mare taught me otherwise. I learned to press into God for healing. Sounds strange, I know. God taught me to believe for more. Much more.

Horseback riding is dangerous. Injuries inevitable. Today's mishap caused two injured knees. The right knee was quite painful. The left knee tolerable. I laid hands on the seriously injured right knee and began to pray, "There will be NO swelling, NO pain, NO bruising, and NO repercussions. In Jesus' name."

Even if I flinched, I thanked God for His healing. In a couple of days, the right knee returned to normal. Can't say the same for the left knee.

Originally, I approached the minor agitation with "it'll be just fine" attitude. Tormented by a dull throb on the less than perfect joint, I resort to massaging the left knee, proclaiming, "Ouch, it hurts."

Six weeks pass before the pain left. "Okay Lord. What was that all about?!"

The soft voice explains, *"You came in agreement with the pain, not the healing. The principle of agreement works no matter which direction applied."*

Smack down!! This epiphany revolutionized my life!

LIFE IS MESSY

There's no getting around it

R-E-L-I-E-F

Diversion only delays the inevitable. Life goes cattywampus when trust is violated. Trust is nearly impossible to repair.

Here it is, the Tuesday before Thanksgiving, and I'm standing before a judge charged with an "unwanted touch" by the man I married all those years ago. How bizarre is that?

They call it a hearing, but really trust is on trial.

The heavy-handed gavel slams the bench. The painful sentence is imposed: "Six weeks of domestic violence classes."

I should be grateful. Instead, a spark is ignited! That man, soon to be an ex, threw his wife into the slammer! And only the naughty one is ordered to attend domestic violence classes?!

Fire purifies and reveals what's hidden beneath the surface. All of us are capable of the unimaginable when pushed to the edge, even good Sunday school teachers like me.

How did nearly thirty years of marriage land in the toilet?

Over time, money became an issue. You could say I resented the ten pairs of cowboy boots Ben purchased at once while I carried all the household expenses. It's true. Why should I support a man who hasn't spoken to me in years? You must be joking? He merely used me. Blood boils.

Look at our account balances; you'll see who should press who for maintenance!

Divorce is UGLY. None can deny it. Hear tell, amicable divorces do exist. The decision to end our lengthy marriage was not taken lightly. The long-suffering one could bear the silence no more.

In my world, communication equates to value. A woman needs to be valued, loved, and appreciated. Men need respect. Both elements were missing in our marriage for a long time.

To intentionally withhold your spouse's needs is abusive. Unfortunately, this only came to light in the heat of the struggle.

We never discussed contentious issues. Instead, we swept trouble under the rug. Did we assume resolution magically appears? Or troubles just vaporize? In retrospect, yes is the answer to both questions.

Silence is a powerful sword to wield. Not until later would its effects come to light. To ignore people is to say they have no value, not worthy of time or attention. Even the most tenacious ego can be stomped out, demeaned, debilitated, and altered.

Confidence is fragile. I say this not for pity or sympathy but to open eyes. As awful as it sounds, we've all done it—at work, in the neighborhood, at church. It's cruel. Everyone has worth and purpose.

Divorce does not erase pain. In fact, afterward the depths of heartache begin to surface. This is not a "don't do it" speech if you are contemplating divorce. I'm just being honest about the process. Studies show the rate of marriage survival decreases with each divorce.

For Ben, I'm number three. Lucky me.

You might think this is all about me, but you too can be free. Never was it my intention to print this story. The Lord impressed upon me, *"many people experience similar heartache."*

May this story impart the same freedom given to me.

Shame is a chokehold. Life is messy. Satan is the accuser. Not God. God sets the captives free. He is our deliverer.

For those who have endured divorce only to have well-meaning Christians beat them up, this chapter is for you. You know the cruel words I'm talkin' about. People left the church over the divorcee Sunday school teacher remaining in position.

All I can say, "Take the log out of your own eye before you try to pull the splinter out of your brother's (Matthew 7:5).

Divorce is spelled R-E-L-I-E-F.

Relief wraps me as a warm blanket. Ending the constant undermining, silence, and belittling.

The idea of remarriage nauseates me. Arrows of judgment from religious ones pierce my heart.

My head spins. I need to scripturally sort this out.

"I know what the Word says about divorce and remarriage, but God, what do you say?"

The Spirit's voice whispers, *"I divorced and took on another."*

WOW! Knock me over with a feather! The church does NOT teach this. How profound! For those who struggle, check out Jeremiah 3:8 to see if it's not true.

Nowhere in the Bible is divorce called a sin. Nowhere. However, that does not give license for *partner rotation.*

God hates divorce, so do I. Who enjoys pain?

Divorce cripples and destroys relationships beyond just the two of you. Repercussions of divorce run deep. Children, friends, family, all of society, for that matter, suffers.

"How did this happen?" you ask.

Buckle up! It's quite the story.

The Trap

Passive-aggressive wears a victim badge. You've seen it raise its ugly head and hiss. It's not gender specific. We all know someone; maybe we are that one.

Blindsided. My entire wardrobe sprawls on the office floor!

Keyless, I stand at the door in shock. Our bedroom boasts a new lockset. Confrontation is inevitable.

Coiled in the chair, the venomous snake preps to snare. Aiming to catch every word, a tape recorder is held firmly in his hand. He waves it about, as if to shout, "Gotcha now!"

911 waits for Ben's call.

This ambush bears the earmarks of a conniving lawyer!

"Oh Reneé, there you go speculating, how would you know?"

Because my own lawyer made the identical suggestion. That's how. What a sly business generator. Ingenious really. Win-win on both sides. For lawyers anyway.

Our daughter's previous courtroom experience educated me to one simple fact, the person who throws the first punch is the loser.

The perturbed wife refrains from a beat down! Options run through my mind. The choice was made. Not necessarily the right one, but I considered it the safest of all choices.

The hostile wife discovered that she should NEVER underestimate the repercussions of sitting on her husband's lap and brushing his ballcap.

Did I want to hurt him? Oh yeah! And not just a little bit.

Snake's ballcap was the intended target, really. My hand barely brushed his slithering forehead.

Hear tell, people go to jail for such outrageous behavior.

Find your groove. Relationships need to be nourished. Marriage takes two to revitalize or stab to death. Both demand time and attention. Hurting people hurt people.

No one steps away blameless.

Despite how victimized I felt, it was imperative to figure out *my* part of a failed marriage. The bitter truth became crystal clear: *Reneé* is a hardcore enabler. There, I said it! I created this pathetic man whom I now resent. Ben was dependent on me.

Note to self: Figure out why you enable.

Woman, somebody should slap some sense into you!

NOW STOP IT!

Men in Blue

Ben used to be fond of lap sitting.

Guess who's handcuffed and hauled off like a criminal? That's right! For lap sitting! I know. Unbelievable. Okay, maybe the slap had something to do with it, but the intended target was his ballcap. It's not like I bit the wicked snake's head off.

Look for joy in the storm. If you can't find it, create it. No sense in allowing a rare opportunity like this to go to waste. Some might consider my response peculiar, but it's what I do. Unsolicited advice is offered to my silent escort in blue. Some fresh ideas could enhance the police department's image.

To start with, "The squad car's seats could use warmers," coming from a backseat perspective of course. "Hot tempers could be soothed. Just sayin'."

Now, it's understandable why these seats are soooo hard. Makes for easier clean up. Another thing, "Talk to your handcuffed detainees. We are real people. Not everyone in handcuffs has a propensity for violent behavior." Remember, we are innocent until proven guilty.

Must you confiscate my shoes to take delicate fingerprints? "Those shoes won't fit you." Tile floors are cold. As a pleasant gesture, might the handcuffed one suggest warm fuzzy booties? No doubt you don't want detainees to catch cold while enjoying your fine hospitality.

"Those eyeglasses won't look good on your face either." Of course, they pay no mind to my goofy comments. All this precaution seems overkill. Maybe men in blue have been fooled by slippery prisoners. But what do I know? Until today, I was a law-abiding citizen, not a loathsome criminal.

Monday evenings must be slow, as I'm the sole tenant in the pristine cell. This is quite an adventure for a gal who doesn't get out much.

Challenged by the somber demeanor of the officer who keeps peeking through the mini blinds, I cannot resist. Can this jailbird get men in blue to crack a smile? I love a challenge. Grab the opportunity when presented. You never know if you'll get another chance. The songbird draws from her nitty-gritty soulful self and recounts the famous biblical jailbreak and belts out a brand-new song:

Paul and Silas in the county jail

They were waitin' for their bail.

Oh, Paul and Silas in the county jail,

They were waitin' for their bail.

Praisin'! That's what they were doing,

Was praisin' almighty God.

Oh, Paul and Silas in the county jail,

They were waitin' for their bail.

Sadly, the men in blue never flinched. They could've chuckled. Poor sports.

Eyes of admiration frequently peered between the closed mini blinds, keeping watch on the one-hit-wonder on the other side of the bulletproof glass. Star struck police have outdone themselves, capturing a genuine fruitcake.

I'm used to it. No doubt the paparazzi seek a photo opp. Oh, that's right, they already have it. If singing jailbirds are not their forte, the cell's acoustical design should have been reconsidered.

AMAZING. I've never sounded so good. It must be the tile. Impressive as I was, the gig is up. Two a.m., pastor sprung the singing canary from captivity.

One might ask, "Why are you airing your dirty laundry?"

No one's above finding themselves in this position. You could be next. Should you ever find yourself behind bars, you are now armed with serious pointers. You're welcome.

If jail is shameful to you, lend me your ear. There's more.

Three days later, the amusement of the caper wore off. Now you tell me, if sitting in the slammer doesn't wipe self-righteousness off your holy heinie, what will?

"Murder?"

Murder Anyone?

Passion plays into the hands of bitterness. It only begins to describe my state of being. A slap will hardly suffice. Rage consumes this mortal body. I'm talking bloodthirsty, murderous, revengeful rage.

Do you recall the movie *Chicago*? Its timing was impeccable. The song, "He Had It Coming!" plays over and over in my head, feeding my thirst for blood.

It didn't help when the news covered a dentist accidentally running over her cheatin' husband multiple times in her Mercedes. That's right, the "accident" happened outside their upscale honeymoon hotel.

Blissful memories altered forever.

Then I had a dream. In this dream I purchased a firearm. Now, I've never owned or even shot a gun. Yet, there I was, practicing at the firing range. My steely unwavering eye is fixed on the target.

Bulls-eye!

Convinced the entrapment of days prior was the attorney's doing. Revenge clothed a cold, cold heart and steady hand. Neither Ben nor his lawyer will escape my wrath. Justice will be served. No matter the cost. My dream concludes.

Shaken and scared by the depths of my raging cold heart, I call my friend. "Pray for me! I want to kill Ben and his attorney." No advice or judgment, only a prayer given for the revenge seeker.

After we hang up, the Spirit of God begins to reason with me. *"Life is full of choices. You can choose to kill your husband and spend the rest of your life in prison. Your daughter will be parentless. Or you can choose not to kill him. It's your freedom on the line. Those female inmates you met* on Sunshine's prison tour, they will be your new best friends. Is that really what you want? It's your choice."

Anger or hatred does not begin to hold a candle to rage. Rage is all-consuming, never experienced before by this Sunday school teacher.

The Lord made some valid points. The outraged one takes a deep breath and a huge leap of faith.

The war began. A battle of a lifetime! Not between spouses, but the war on rage. Every passing minute I had to choose *not* to succumb to murderous, blood-thirsty, revenge-seeking rage.

Choice is a super power.

Not to make this all about me, but life in prison was on the line. Sunshine's parentless future hangs in the balance. Selfish? You bet! The sword of decision is hurled. Engaged in hand-to-hand combat with death itself. A fight to spare the head of the snake I married all those years ago and his loathsome attorney.

Three grueling days of brutal conflict subside. Victorious warrior clothed in God's mercy remains. Exhausted from the warfare. Hungry for vindication.

This wife didn't deserve to go to jail. Nor did she deserve to be used and ignored all those years. What does one do when betrayal made the mark?

"Lord, I'd appreciate a little vindication here. I was sooo wronged. I want my name cleared."

Clear as day, the Spirit of God spoke: *"I'll give you vindication. Ben will live with the decisions he has made."*

Now if that doesn't bend a kink in your neck, I'm not sure what will. The Lord's words resonated loudly. Mind you, His interpretation of vindication was not envisioned by this warrior, but I'm okay, even at peace, with His plan.

Talk to Me God, Before I Slap Somebody!

What an unexpected form of justice from my God, my Advocate!

If it hadn't been for His reasoning with this determined wife, *Talk to Me God, Before I Slap Somebody!* would have been written from behind bars, with a more nefarious title.

Gratitude swells.

God saved me and yes two others from a deadly outcome.

∞∽

To know yourself is to walk in shoes on fire.

Until then, it's pure speculation.

Note to self: I am not a victim, but I am victorious, an overcomer, a master of choice.

> *If you do not forgive others their sins,*
> *your father will not forgive your sins. (Mark 11:25)*

SMOLDERING

Rocky Mountain National Park

Felt sorry for myself one dark hour,
when the Spirit of God said,
*"Reneé, take authority over that spirit.
Don't let it continue to harass you."*

Out of the Fire

The temperature was risin'
The flames unbearably hot
Asphyxiating smoke consumes me
My friends just stand and watch
As this flesh of mine sizzles and pops

I knew not who I was
This time she has gone too far
Others plainly expressed
Crossed the line of no return
Where is the woman we once knew?

Finished
Washed up
Lost for all eternity
The words and comments flew

The verdict was made, after all
Only an ash heap remained
Or so it seemed
Then out of the rubble
My life was redeemed

The image is all different
Than the one before
With its edges all charred and scored

An inner beauty not seen by man
Arose from the ash
Different from before

No longer willing to judge
Knowing not where people have been
Strange as it seems
It was all part of God's plan

To burn off self-righteousness
Replacing it with a heart of compassion
I'd do it all over again
Enduring the flames
Just to see the benefit it brings

Trouble in the Paddock

During the tumultuous season before the divorce was finalized, I lived in the basement of our home. There was no surplus of funds. After all, divorce costs money. Lots of money.

"Wasn't it uncomfortable?"

"Absolutely!"

A girl's gotta do what a girl's gotta do. Suck it up buttercup! Battle on. This too shall pass.

The minute Annette swung open the salon door and waved the postcard with a shout, "I found your house!!" I knew it was true. Filled with anticipation, between appointments, Annette and I rushed over to see the blond brick home advertised on the postcard.

Smitten I was.

My desired home had to meet some major criteria: affordable horse property near work *and* riding trails. Now try that impossible combination right in the heart of town. This property qualifies on all levels! Not just one trailhead but *two* equine parks down the street and only minutes from the salon!

"Lord, is it mine?"

"I've saved it for you."

Peace replaces anguish.

This sweet house was in litigation for three years after the owner's death. That's right, three years! It just cleared the courts. But don't think for a second it was smooth sailing just because the Lord saved it for me.

The Lord instructs, *"Hold off placing an offer."*

Really? Who am I to question God? So, I hold off. Six days later, an inner release comes.

Now I have competition! *What was God thinkin'?* A contractor stirred the pot with another offer. Both offers return to the drawing board for reconsideration.

"Lord, I can climb only so far!"

The seller's bottom dollar was a stretch, at the top of my ability to pay. This cowgirl wannabe waits on pins and needles to hear the results of negotiations.

No idea what the competitive offer looked like, but I'm here to tell you, I'm under contract! This charming house is mine!! To be the proud owner of a fifty-year-old blond, one-owner, well-built brick home with enough room for two horses is heavenly!

No, there is no barn or fence. That doesn't matter.

The Lord saved this home *for me!*

There's more to the skinny.

Annette's client tells me her son has a barn he wants to get rid of. Who do you know wants to get rid of a barn? For free! Her son tried to donate it to a horse rescue, but they won't return his calls.

"I'll take it," I blurt out.

"No. He wants a tax deduction. But I'll mention it to him." The client holds steady on her son's behalf.

"NO" never stood in my way before. Following a discussion with Pastor Stan, the son donates his barn to my small church. He receives a tax write off; the church gets a barn. Fellow parishioners dismantle and move all the pieces, then reassemble the barn in my backyard. I donate a stash of cash to the church for their help, and everyone is happy.

Go figure, the ingenuity of some!

Corral panels and a hitching post pave the way for all things wild and fun.

For the first time in my life, I have a sense of vulnerability. If one lives with horses, one could get injured and no one would know. Time to meet the neighbors.

Horse lovers abound. Comfort surrounds. A high school riding candidate lives at the end of the block. Halfway to her home lives a policeman and his 911 operator wife. The couple attend the same church where I received healing of my legs years earlier.

Two Belgiam horses consume their backyard. Oh mercy, what a glorious barn they have. It's large enough to house a carriage, a hay wagon and all their tack! If I were the envious type—which I'm tempted to be right now—I'd say their barn makes mine look tacky. Most certainly their barn cost a whale of a lot more. Perspective adjustment! What magnificent barns we both have. We are so blessed.

It's giddy-up time. Cody and Buddy will love the lush backyard. Knee-high grass is heavenly compared to last year's dry bales. No matter how grand all this wonderfulness sounds, it's only a third of an acre.

Sipping fresh brew at the kitchen window, the wannabe cowgirl romantically watches two majestic creatures graze in the backyard. Could life be any better?

Fewer flies I suppose. Slap that city girl! It's hard to believe she didn't expect flies.

Two weeks have passed since the horses joined this dreamy homestead. Before retiring for the evening, I glance through the kitchen window. Startled at what I see, Cody is wildly kicking up a storm, struggling to rise from the ground.

This is not a therapeutic back rub!

The dreaded colic! Not like an infant's nagging cough, no, far more serious. A constant diet of fresh grass is the culprit. A horse rolling continuously will result in intestine strangulation, a cause of death.

It's imperative Cody stands up!

HORRIFIED, I rush to Cody's side and fall to my knees. "CODY, GET UP!" Pushing her backside with all my might. "YOU HAVE TO GET UP! YOU CAN'T DIE ON ME NOW, GIRL!"

I sprint down the street to my 911 neighbor. BAM! BAM! BAM! Practically knocking down her door. Dogs hysterically sound the alarm. In a panic I cry, "Come on! Come on!"

Finally, a sleepy-eyed, tousle-headed day sleeper appears. "Reneé, what's wrong?"

Choking back tears of trauma, "Cody's down. I can't get her up! Help me please."

"Give me a minute, I'll be right over."

In the twilight I dart back to Cody. Her fitful toss continues. Terrified midnight eyes pierce directly into my soul. I push her backside again and again.

"CODY, GET UP!" I wail, frightened I might lose her.

The neighbor arrives. Desperately I muddle through the lump caught in my throat. "She won't get up."

We drop to our knees and with all our might together push on Cody.

"Reneé, lay hands on her and pray! Come on, pray. YOU KNOW HOW! DO IT!"

She does not pray, at least not out loud. She makes me pray. She's right. I know how. I lost my head, wailing instead of doing. *Get a grip Reneé and pray!*

Quivering words muddle through fearful tears, "In Jesus' name, Cody walk in health. Rise. Intestines straighten out. Be normal." I sob, "You will not die Cody. In Jesus' name."

I scarcely finish praying when Cody rolls over and rises to her feet. The waterworks let go. I'm stunned. Like clockwork written for a movie, my incredible neighbor's husband shows up.

What a blur of emotions. He grabs Cody's rope and begins to walk her, then hands her over. "Now you walk her. Keep her moving. Don't let her go down. Keep her on her feet."

The three of us pace the street. An hour of walking passes before the horse wrangler officer feels Cody is out of danger.

What a grueling lifesaving experience.

"Thank You, Lord, for sparing Cody's life and new friends willing to help. Thank You, Lord."

Hotel Strange

What does a single woman do for fun over the holidays? Well, she goes to the hills to soak. That's what she does!

Certainly, the springs will have last-minute hotel vacancies. Silly girl. Hot Sulfur Springs has two hotel options not connected to the pools: a respectable establishment on the highway, a bit pricy for my budget, and one just the other side of the bridge.

A call is made, "Save me a room, I'll be right over."

"Honey, there's no hurry. It'll be here when you're finished at the springs."

"I don't want to take the chance. I'll be over in a couple of minutes."

"Okay, sweetie."

What a strange conversation.

While waiting to be greeted, I poke around. Near the entry is a showcase proudly displaying a newspaper article from twenty years earlier of the gentleman from New York who purchased the Hot Springs Hotel. You guessed it, the Hotel I'm attempting to check into. Aren't I the nosy one? Nosy moseys toward the curled old newspaper article featuring the eccentric man from New York who purchased the nostalgic hotel twenty years earlier.

You guessed it, the hotel I'm attempting to check into.

Am I trespassing into someone's personal space? Nosy Rosey peeks around the corner to see two gentlemen sitting in the dimly lit living room, glued to daytime soaps. An eternity passes before the show ends and a tall, skinny, grey-haired fella jumps up to assist the patient hotel guest.

"Hello, there. Are you the one who called?" he asks.

"Yes. Yes, I am."

"Let me show you your room."

His hunchbacked companion, Igor, remains undisturbed, fixed on the screen. The living room fireplace crackles as we pass. Strange holiday décor oozes from every spare inch.

The face pictured in the newspaper article is a much younger Ricardo. He leads me up the creaky staircase to explore the room options.

"Now these rooms have private baths. They cost extra."

Budget friendly is my priority.

Richardo nonchalantly warns, "Please be discreet, should you need to streak across the hallway naked in the middle of the night."

Although his crude comment is meant to be comical, it is creepy. Does this guy peep through keyholes? Each room's doorway is open. Room keys lay on top of the nightstands. I chose the room nearest the bathroom.

No other guest? It's early I justify.

A tall skinny Santa rests on a rickety old chair at the bottom of the stairs. "He's sure cute" I comment, not thinking how he resembles the hotel owner.

"You're free to take him to your room if you like. Just don't defile him," Ricardo jests, as if nothing odd is said.

Horrified, I gasp.

"Will you be joining us for dinner?" Ricardo inquires.

Dinner with Igor and the CREEPY hotelier!! Are you kidding??

"Thanks, but no. I don't know how late I'll be at the springs."

Money and pleasantries are exchanged, and I leave, not sure what just happened. Bizarre indeed.

Shortly thereafter, soaking in the hot springs, two local ladies engage in conversation, "Where are you staying?"

"At Hotel Strange."

"Ooooo, Ricardo. He's creepy. If you don't feel safe, call me. My number is in the phone book. I'll put you up overnight."

Yikes, if you don't feel safe? Slap me silly! What have I gotten myself into? Nothing about this discussion puts me at ease. If the people in town think Ricardo is creepy, there must be a reason.

Strategizing all the way back I think, I'll sneak into the room so as not to be seen. Yeah. That's what I'll do. Quietly, I open the door adjacent to the restaurant. Dishes clang in rhythm. Dinner guests chatter over white table linens. Sure smells good. Ricardo and Igor are too busy serving to notice the likes of me.

Whew! Catastrophe dodged.

The wet babe runs upstairs. Only the skinny Santa Claus knew she returned. And he wasn't tellin'.

Just in case someone might peek through a keyhole, the scared one quickly jumps into bed, throws the covers over her head to warm up and proceeds to journal, documenting this very strange experience in the event she doesn't live to see daylight.

Sometime after I fell asleep, the ruckus of arriving guests abruptly awakened the scared one. Consumed with strange thoughts like witnesses are a great deterrent. Not wanting to become a victim. After all, this experience could shift me to become a murder mystery writer, should I live to tell the tale.

I pray for peace and above all, protection.

Daylight dawns. Whew! What a night! I live to sing another song and write another poem. Do I dare cross over for a shower? Braveheart silently tiptoes across the hallway, brushes her teeth, and prepares for a new day. Down the stairs I bounce, greeted by a skinny winking Santa.

"Hey, Ricardo, where can a gal get a cup of coffee around here?"

"I've got a fresh pot in the kitchen, come on."

Trailing Ricardo through the kitchen. He dispenses piping hot coffee from an exquisite new-fangled commercial stainless brew dispensary into a white porcelain cup.

This morning Ricardo has an entirely different demeanor, a far less scary, more pleasant character. Where was this guy yesterday?

Ricardo chuckles, "When people from back East ask directions, I send them on a wild goose chase through town."

"Now why would you do that?" The town is only a few blocks wide and not much longer.

"They won't believe me otherwise," Ricardo shrugs. "Hey, you should come back on New Year's Eve. We're having a big party!"

"Sounds like fun. Count me out. Thanks anyway."

Somebody should slap Ricardo to the moon and back! What a trip. Second thought, he might like it.

Sidenote: Sorry to say, though the building still stands, Hotel Strange is no more. Ricardo and Igor were a peculiar but memorable experience. This encounter still creeps me out and makes me laugh at the same time.

All Cracked Up

Dating was filled with rejection, betrayal, lies, and heartache, much like a marriage gone rogue. Don't get me wrong, I became engaged to a guy after knowing him only six weeks. Yes, it was stupid. That's what starvation for love does. Makes 'em do stupid.

Singleness is not all it's cracked up to be, at least not for me.

Romance clouds perspective. TV romanticizes the single life. My viewpoint could be altered by an occasional date.

eHarmony boasts they have a match for everyone, but they didn't for me. I'm special. Match.com let me know only a very small percentage of men are interested in my type. Great! Add that to a decaying self-image and there lies a crumpled-up mess! Sigh.

I dangle the "Free Condo" lure. "Join me in Frisco over the Fourth of July for fireworks and a parade." Girls stay over. Boys go home. My condo. My rules.

Nothing like a small-town celebration! Tents line the streets with trinkets. Delicious aromas drift amongst the crowd.

Hurry! The parade is about to begin! Whistles and hoopla erupt over the mass of tricycles, bicycles, children, and dogs. Streamers, toys, and all things red, white, and blue flutter in the breeze from helmets, handlebars, and pets.

Home-grown soldiers in uniform pass by. It's such an honor to be in the presence of warriors who sacrifice so much. The enthusiastic crowd cheers, claps, and whistles while I cry.

Moments like this move me so. Does it affect you like this? Whenever the national anthem is sung or played, even if by beginners, this crybaby is a mess. Freedom does that to me.

Sparkling red firetrucks are always a big hit. Pumped with enthusiasm, the crowd waves at small children tossing candy, straddling their daddy hunks. Obviously, well-known heroes.

Appreciation floods my soul for our local firefighters. Again, the waterworks flow.

Quick! Dodge or get wet. The mob screams in delight. High-powered water guns drench the scorched crowd. Now that's COOL advertisement to entice enthusiasm for river rafting!

The best of show must go to the shiny orange Flight for Life helicopter. Spectators go wild as the helicopter swoops over the rescue trucks. These are our guys and gals. Woot! Woot!

What a grand finale!

No, WAIT! Would you look at that! Clanging pans dangle off an ol' mule alongside a quintessential mountain man.

Under the straggly fur hat protrudes an old bearded fella dressed in grubby, hand-sewn, fringed leather coat and pants. His shoulders are draped in tattered fur pelts.

As quickly as the mule and mountain man appear, they vanish.

Now that's a small-town mountain parade! Real people. Real characters. Real fun.

If a parade and sizzlin' hot temps don't whet an appetite for white water rafting, not certain what will. My friend Lisa has come up to the mountain, and that's exactly what we chose to do!

Arkansas Run Wild

On the banks
Of the Arkansas River we stand
Ready for our leader
To give us the command

All the blue rafts
In the shoot ready to go
Like a stampede
They catch the flow

"Lord, protect and keep us safe
Who knows the dangers
We're about to embrace"

As the crack of a whip
Flung the words
"Paddle right! Paddle hard!
Keep up with the herd"

The major attraction for the day
Is the Toilet Bowl Flush
It's coming our way

PADDLE HARD!
PADDLE FAST!
Hang on to your hats

Get ready to ride
The raging rapids want to eat us alive

Lean in! Lean in!
Came the call
With stern warning
Lest you fall

The blue raft
Bucked a time or two
Then out of the saddle
This cowgirl flew

Yet remain all six
Of the other buckaroos
What happened next
Is a slow-motion flash
As time quickly began to pass.

Painted pink toes rose to the air
Blindly trying to locate downstream
not knowing where

Buckaroos were concerned
As she slid under the boat
Up top a shuffle dance occurred
While Jeremy tried to lasso the herd

Adrenaline kicks in
Sharp as a tack, quick on his feet
Came to my rescue
Our commander-in-chief

High centered we became
Needing to be rescued
once again

He said he was fine
But I read his face
As the rapids bashed him
And pinned him in the most precarious place

Once again, we were on our way
Bursting forth in laughter
"Ye Haw!"
Came the shout of relief for the day

Credit all goes to the head wrangler dude
Jeremy
To whom I owe much gratitude

The Arkansas River runs wild
And so do those who try
To ride the treacherous rapids
For them
The adventure will never die

Little did I know a day of salvation and serious baptism was in store! What a rush! Jeremy saved my life!

I burst out in jovial laughter. Strange I know. It's how I roll.

Farley

One discriminating widower is willing to romp through Breckenridge on the Fourth of July with this wild thing. It's been difficult. Office mates don't engage with Richard since he lost his wife. Pitiful. Engineers are an odd sort.

Through hordes of posh festival booths, we meander.

"I've spent years searching for a powerful dancer," Richard divulges. "It can be an oiled bronze, a painting, or an abstract. But it needs to exude power and movement."

We scour for hours before stopping in our tracks.

"Oh, my!" She takes our breath away. Our eyes feast upon the life-sized Spanish dancer in motion. Shades of red swoop off the canvas! "She is lovely!"

She's propped up on the easel as the artisan makes his final touches. So lifelike. Spellbound we are. As if her ballerina skirt touched us in the twirl.

Richard steps aside and watches the savvy shopper negotiate for the masterpiece. He just can't come to grips with spending that much money. Oh, well.

Shopping is exhausting. Heat makes one thirsty.

Richard says, "Breckenridge is too busy. Let's do lunch in Frisco."

"Let's go."

Rich and Renée at Farley's in Breckenridge

On the corner of Main and Fifth sits a quaint bistro. Who could resist Farley's abundant flowers overflowing the rail and intimate patio? A beckoning lure. Before our food arrives, a musician silently sets up in the corner, strums his guitar, and serenades the small audience. Relish the unexpected romantic moment.

Can't help but notice the miserable couple at the table across the aisle—they exchange no conversation, no eye contact, nor show any interest in one another.

"They're married," I comment.

"How can you tell?"

"I recognize the signs. Silence and no eye contact."

"That's a horrible commentary on marriage! Bobbi's and mine was never in such a state."

"Mine was."

Between the musician and traffic, it's a struggle to overcome background noise. Inching a little closer, "Ouch!" I jerk my smashed finger from the iron patio chair. Richard reaches over, covers my hand and prays for the flattened finger.

"Oh, my!" A moment for pause. Romance sparks could fly if one was so inclined. *Sigh.* Wishful thinking. No date followed. Bummer.

Five months later . . .

Christmas sneaks up. Holidays wrap themselves in expectation to accommodate our happiness. *Self, in lieu of wallowing in self-pity, throw a Christmas party!* Invite a bunch of singles. Christmas decorations hung. Fragrance of food and pine, love and laughter fill both home and soul.

What a fabulous cure. *Sigh.*

Jesus' birthday, a joyful cause for reflection. Life is sweet. That is until Christmas Eve. Stood up by a date! How can anyone be so rude? Didn't Stu's mama teach him manners? You know what Stu needs? Yep.

"God, you told me to give this guy another chance. Look what happened! Do you realize I turned down dinner with friends on Christmas Eve for a lousy no-show date?"

Suck it up, buttercup. Singlehood is not for wimps. It smarts! Repeated betrayals compounded by deep rejection could cause pitiful ones to drown. *People are dying all around the world, and here I am wallowing in self-pity! STOP IT!*

It's hard to see ourselves objectively. Girl, get your panties out of a wad. Accept it; you're not ordinary. You're outspoken, uninhibited, and possess a twisted sense of humor.

It could be worse. I could be an axe murderer, a slug, or worse, a dreadful cook! Get over your bad self!

Heart Massage

Awe …
To massage another's heart
Requires trust and time
Tender loving care
And gentle hands
If you plan to go there

It is not to be treated lightly
The massage of the heart
But with privilege
And respect
Not knowing where it's been
It could be rather tender
and bruised deep within

When the proper attention
Is given to the heart
It will blossom with love
And the ability to impart

That is the benefit and beauty
Of massaging another one's heart

Honky-Tonk

Evidently, life unfolds at eighteen. By simply turning a calendar page, underdeveloped brains suddenly turn into responsible adults. Fascinating.

That philosophy drove my domineering father's decisions, as dating was forbidden before the ripe age of eighteen.

I could be dead by then. Call it spite, call it stupid, call it rebellious, call it whatever you want, instead of dating, I got married.

That didn't go over well.

It's tough to find your groove after being out of circulation since fifteen. As if I ever had one.

Eighteen months have passed since the dreadful life-altering jailbreak. This now single babe decides to wade out. Country line-dancing is a good place to start. No date required.

Several ladies meet at the *Grizzly Rose* on occasion. It's the biggest, baddest honky-tonk saloon in town where a girl can cut loose. Short flippin' skirts and high fashion cowgirl boots are a girl's uniform on the dance floor.

Line dancing beats a lonely Saturday night at home. Miss Sassy is not seeing anyone. Praying friends are responsible. No doubt, they speculate trouble will follow if I'm left to my wild self.

Sigh. It might be true. How would I know. Up to this point, it's not been tested.

The rustic saloon is packed. Walls are papered with well-groomed and perfumed bodies. Tables host purses, drinks, and a watch dog.

Ah, there's a spot. "See it? Look!" Pointing to the only empty spot on the rail. "I can fit there!"

Boots are scootin', heads are bobbin', skirts are twirlin', synchronized to a well-rehearsed country-western band. Mesmerized I am!

Swanky cowboys dressed to impress strut their tight pressed jeans and fancy cowboy hats. Beer flows at the bar. Flashy boots glide over the wooden dance floor.

Swaying to the band playing "Neon Moon," I sashay my way to join the toe tappers against the rail. Before the song ends, I'm overtaken by a strange sense.

Miss Sassy glances to the right. Not a soul for ten to fifteen feet. I glance to the left. All the beautiful people have cleared the crowded rail! Discreetly as one standing alone in front of a crowd can be, I check my armpits. A shower was had. Everything seems fresh.

How bizarre is this? Why has everyone fled? Hmmm.

The stark realization hits, *Self, you don't belong here. There ain't no honky-tonk, boot scootin' boogie to be had by the likes of you. Not tonight anyway.*

Chap my hide! PARTY GIRL DENIED! I'm tempted to hurt somebody, but NOOO! Slap happy is restrained.

Girl, you cannot deny the results of praying friends. UGH!

Follow the Lead

"What does a good match look like?" Whether a home or companion, there are striking similarities. They come in all shapes, sizes, colors, and locations. Not to mention leaky pipes. Whether a playdate or a place to permanently hang your hat, there're plenty of options.

Upgrades? Well, that's a bit more complicated. Attention to detail is imperative.

Days of dreaming Mr. Right will arrive on the scene like a Hallmark movie are gone. Hear tell, love is found on-line.

Hours are spent answering endless personal questions on multiple dating apps. Minutes later a response pops up!

"There is no one for you." Hard to believe. I know. I know.

Dating sites are like a smorgasbord feasting on fear of missing out. Why commit to pot roast or lemon pie? Piping hot and more delicious could arrive soon. Struggle, meet overindulgence, commitment phobias' perfect match.

What do fussy eaters do? Pick through desserts? Settle for ordinary? Overindulge? Starved for love, the endless buffet grows wearisome. I want more. Not more men, silly, but a real relationship.

Ballroom dance lessons are promising. A time of exploration beyond the obvious. Dance is not merely rhythmic hip movement and coordinated steps. Gentlemen develop leadership skills and ladies learn to follow.

Ladies, it's all about framework. No man can direct a limp noodle. Give him frame. Help him lead you. Tell him.

Men, give that gal a firm lead. How can we follow if you're lost? Don't ruthlessly whip on her. She doesn't like that, and you look like a-a-a donkey.

Incredible how this lead-follow routine comes in handy. For example, choir, don't just start singing; watch the director's lips and cue. Now follow. Stay in unison. Or at work, follow the boss's directives. Sounds so simplistic.

Harsh reality for such an independent woman. Instinctively, I lead, so to follow, well let's just say, Ms. Independent could stand some pointers. Redemptive qualities should follow dance lessons.

Gentlemen are supposed to lead. Girl power is so prominent today. For so long, men have been pushed aside and beat down. If given freedom to do so, he'll rise to the occasion.

You want girl power? Let me slap you! Don't rule over him. Give him back his power.

Men, treat her kindly, lead her gently yet firmly, and she will follow on and off the dance floor (consider this a bonus).

Personal advisors instruct Ms. Independent, "Be realistic. Lower your expectation. Keep those sought-after qualities or deal breakers under ten."

Really? Why? If you expect nothing, guess what you get?

Ten qualifications are not nearly enough. I refuse to settle for less. I've already had the other.

Compatibility is imperative for older start-ups. Focus on similarities not differences. Don't expect someone to fill the gap of your lack. Would you want that kind of pressure?

How's this for a pick-up line? "Hey baby, are you the one willing to do what I won't?" Don't be ridiculous. If you want someone to compensate for your *weak spots,* I suggest you work on your bad self!

Note to self: To avoid a repeat, explore your part of the failed marriage.

Can you even believe I'm wanting a man after all I've gone through? I know. I can't either. Is it in our DNA?

Not that my opinion matters, but later in life, if you haven't grown used to your differences while young, they become an irritant.

As you have rightfully concluded, there are few eligible prospects who meet my standards. Compromise is not part of this girl's makeup. Sound outrageous? I know.

No wise friend dares set me up. Instead, they petition the Lord on my behalf for protection. It works too. You saw what happened at the *Grizzly Rose*.

Dance lessons impact me beyond expectation. They show off my strengths and weakness and the importance of flowing with a partner.

Self, every good leader needs to know how to follow.

This dating cycle is madness. It's been a long five years since the ugly death of my marriage. Rejection still haunts me.

"Lord, deliver me from this turmoil."

"A good friend would be nice, Lord."

That said, I'm over it! Done! The hunt for a meaningful relationship is over!

I mean it! Really, I do.

Pink Flamingo

A profound prayer slips past these un-kissed lips. "Lord, may he be to me what I have need of, and may I be to him, what he has need of. Whoever *him* is."

Since junior high, I've heard the voice of the Lord. These encounters are set apart from any other by their profound personal impact. January sixth is forever etched in my mind as I prayed a simple prayer. "Lord, teach me how to love you, so I'll know how to love a husband."

These prayers transformed my life.

In a quiet voice I hear, *"Let me teach you."*

Well, okay then. Reneé, dig out the pink journal you've saved for something BIG. This qualifies. Inside the front cover, yours truly stamps, *LOVE BOOT CAMP Survival Manual.*

Never in my wildest dreams did I expect to share this intimate chapter of my life. Although, I should have seen it coming when the Lord told me, *"Don't share everything."*

Today, you are a recipient of the spring from which I drink.

If you thirst for more, dive into the pool of living water for yourself. There is plenty for everyone.

Expectation rises. God's principles are universal. Follow along, as I pen God's voice and sometimes my response.

Doubters in the crowd, don't think for a minute my diary is fabricated. By now, you should recognize my voice. This loving, healing voice is *not* mine. Let the flamingo speak for itself.

JANUARY 8
"I'm jealous over you" I want to be first, not a man."

JANUARY 9

Spoken so profoundly through my friend as if I heard His audible voice, *"Men don't like to be told what to do, neither does God! Reneé quit telling God what and how to do things."*

Ouch! But ... "I'm so good at it!" says the experienced one.

JANUARY 10 4:45 A.M.

"Desire spurs intimacy. Rise early to meet Me. The man set aside for you, likes his house in order! I like my house in order!"

This speaks volumes as I'm not the tidiest creature on the planet. "Lord, I feel enrolled in a crash course."

He informs me, *"It is because there's a husband waiting for you. He will love you like no man has ever loved you."*

8 P.M.

"I want you to prepare yourself for Me this evening."

But Lord, I'm tired; I've had a long day.

"And I haven't?"

He makes me laugh. Humor and truth breathes a fresh perspective of who God is.

"My day hasn't been nearly as exhausting as Yours, has it?"

10:10 P.M.

"I like you to smell good. Praise is incense before my nostrils that pleases Me. It will also please your husband. I desire to change the way you see yourself. Don't try to outguess Me or my plans."

JANUARY 11 5 A.M.
"Lord, I'm so tired."

"It's not about you; I need your love, your attention, your praise! I enjoy showing you, you can trust me. I can do all things because you believe in Me! Build Me up before you head out the door. I pull on your strength to get through the day. If you believe in your man, he will strut his stuff to reward you so as to not disappoint you.

You my dear, have the ability to create impossible situations into possibilities by your man strutting his stuff from your praise. This man of yours, my dear, has frailties, you are not to point them out, he is aware of them. You are to encourage him and believe in him. Pray for him, and I will cover him. You empower Me when you believe in Me."

JANUARY 14 6:45 A.M.
The Lord awakens me with a blessing spoken over me. "This morning, My sweet love, I bless you with strength from above, endurance to get through the day and creativity along the way. A hedge of protection to keep you safe. I bless you on high with power and grace."

SUNDAY JANUARY 15 5:20 A.M.

"I bless Your Holy name Lord."

"Now don't go getting religious on Me now! Praise Me from your inner most parts."

"I give You honor, Lord."

"Honor is what you do, not what you say. Respect is the highest regard paid through the way you refer and act towards one. Praise is worship for who I am. Like perfume to your man's nostrils, your praise is to me, a sweet aroma. Praise creates in Me a desire to hold you tightly to My bosom, to smell you. The fragrance of praise comes up before my nostrils and creates desire within Me to do something special for you."

"WOW! WOW! WOW! Blow me out of the water! WOW! What a beautiful picture, Lord."

JANUARY 16 9:20 A.M.

"I create new every day. My mercies are fresh and new as the morning dew served on a platter for you. I deliver to you My rose of Sharon to accompany mercy prepared for you. Enjoy its aroma. It is like no other. Its fragrance will bring healing to your soul."

8:55 P.M.

"Lord, will I be a threat to every man?"

"Not every man, but to most, yes."

Of course, I laugh.

"I do have one reserved for you."

Of course, I must ask, "Who?" (Smiles)

"None of your business. It'll come, don't fret. There is time for that later. First things first. I need to establish who you are in Me before I establish or reestablish whose you are. My timing is perfect."

"Yes, Lord, I trust You."

JANUARY 18 6:30 A.M.
"Don't be so quick to eliminate Richard."

This isn't the first time I've heard this regarding a particular man, so I take it with a grain of salt. "I call upon You as my source. Lord, the source of power, light and understanding, impart into me what I have need of today."

"I will impart into you today not only strength, but courage."

9:12 P.M.
"Tonight, I want you to begin to thank Me for what I have done for you and on your behalf. I desire to dispatch angels to take care of you. Tell Me, darling, what do you desire?"

JANUARY 19 4:35 A.M.
God continues to stretch me and dig deeper to creatively worship Him. "Lord, You are my defender, my protector. You believe in me when all others fall away. I thank You that You think enough to cover me."

"You need lots of defending because you mess up so much. Many have thought you won't make it. I have sent some to stand in your defense."

Sobbing over truth revealed. His comforting words saturate my soul.

"I've told you I will never leave you, nor forsake you. I desire to cleanse you from your pain."

"Please do so, Lord, please do."

"I've healed you from your deep wounds; now, let Me apply pain reliever to the scars to melt them away. Now, release it to Me and let Me have the pain. I'll apply salve and rub it out."

9:42 P.M.

"Lord, what is the plan for tonight? Where are we headed?"

"Worship Me."

"Since you have taken me down this process, I'm not sure how to do that. Teach me, Lord"

"Quietly lay face down and wait for Me. Expect. Listen."

I did as told, and experienced a vision: I saw the throne; the river of life flows from it. I was told to *"drink of the river of life and to come often."*

JANUARY 22 SUNDAY 7 A.M.

"You are a beautiful flower in My garden. You've had a few hailstorms. I need to repair your damaged and bruised petals."

My friend, indulge in another sip before moving on.

"I missed your praise and worship coming before My nostrils. I wondered where My beloved was, the one who

lights my fire. The one who arouses My pleasure sensors was not there. You did not come into My presence yesterday and I missed you."

"I'm sorry, Lord. Who would have thought you'd miss me?"

"I miss all My children, particularly the ones who make themselves known to Me."

Sidenote: During this most intimate time spent with the Lord, I could see the color of His eyes. They are neither blue, green, nor brown. No, they were the color of love.

In the book of Revelation 1:14, it talks about the Lord's eyes being like a flame of fire, which is open for interpretation. Is the flame for us? Does the flame represent anger against His enemies? Could it be both? Or something entirely different?

> *"He heals up the broken hearted and binds up their wounds."*
> *Psalms 147:3*

FRESH START

Morning sunrise in the Beulah Valley

New Day

Sunday, January 22

Headed to church. Radio is off. I hear, *"Respect supersedes all else on your list of desires in a man, other than Me being first."*

Brace for impact! Respect is hard. Yes, it's on my list. Near the bottom. I was thinking, this man needs to be respectful. Never was respect toward him a consideration . . . until now.

Monday, January 23

In lieu of being awakened to more instructions, I'm awakened with a powerful desire to clean house. Dust bunnies disappear; hardwood floors shine. Neatly I tuck the ottoman between its two companions. Scented candles fill the atmosphere. The house smells and looks divine.

Monday is game night. Three out of five attendees are fierce competitors. Two are pleasant participants.

Telephone ring is barely heard over the outburst.

"Hello?"

A polite voice breaks up the chaos, "Reneé, I'd like to bring over the tickets for the play."

"Right now?"

"If that's okay," the familiar voice responds.

"Sure, come on over."

"I'll be there in twenty minutes."

Click. *Twenty minutes, huh? It's a half-hour drive. What's the hurry?* I neglected to disclose the vultures hanging around the dining table. We'll hook him on game night. There will be no escape.

Blood thirsty gamers resume trivia strategy. The doorbell announces our victim's speedy arrival.

"Richard, come on in. Meet my friends."

Eyebrows and speculations rise when playmates hear Richard's name. Now, don't get excited. The only thing they heard was the Lord had told me *"not to be quick to eliminate Richard."* You can only imagine the conclusion this bunch jumped to. Maybe you too.

You remember Christmas Eve, don't you? The Lord told me *"to give that fella a chance"* too. And we know how disappointing that turned out. Expectations are nil.

The minute Richard walked in the house the game lost all appeal. I knew he'd want to talk. After all, he just buried his sister-in-law on the heels of losing his wife a year ago. No doubt the funeral stirred raw emotions. Topic of loss and grief is frequently discussed over haircuts.

"Richard, would you care to talk?"

He pulls back in surprise. "Well, yes! Yes, I would!"

Thankfully, the One who cares about details nudged me into housekeeping this morning.

"Follow me."

Richard follows me down the hall to the nicely arranged room with a delicate hint of gardenia floating in the air. He has my full attention.

"How intuitive you are. I do want to talk. I want to speak to you about us."

Now that was unexpected! "Please, have a seat."

Straight out of the bag, Richard begins to tell the story: "I was at my brother's house in Arizona, lying on the floor half asleep. Puzzle pieces began to fall as snowflakes. Each piece attached to one another. Collectively they formed a picture. That picture was you."

Howdy Doody! Mercy me, I'm blown away!

In dramatic fashion, Richard continues, "Would you be interested in elevating our relationship? Date a couple of times and see if we fit. I will love you like no man has ever loved you."

WOW! Did you hear him? Richard used the exact words the Lord told me! Did you see that coming? I certainly didn't. Knock me over with a feather!

In total shock!! That "I'll love you" line resembles a marriage proposal! We aren't even seeing each other.

Tongue-tied, and short-circuited, I bury myself under the fuzzy throw. I had hoped for a relationship built on friendship before romance, but this is beyond expectation. Richard qualifies as a friend; we've known each other more than seventeen years. Friendships budding into romance are unscripted. The man I respect the most sits directly in front of me and all but proposed!

The Pink Flamingo sessions continue. No longer are we discussing a certain *man*. Instead, we wade deeper into worship. There is nothing that compares to the presence of God. Nothing! Not even an amazing friend, a proposal, a companion, or a spouse.

Our relationship starts off on a peculiar note, then transitions into awkwardly strange when Richard casually comments, "I want to take care of you."

Miss Sassy proclaims, "I don't need no stinkin' man!"

"Well, I don't need no stinkin' woman either!" Richard spars.

Sassy adds, "Let me make this perfectly clear, that doesn't mean I don't want one."

Our Wedding May 6, 2006

He agrees we are on the same page. With that stinkin' business out of the way . . .

Four months later, Richard and I marry.

Serious adjustments are required on the heels of remarriage. Compromise, stretching our comfort zone, for example.

The most difficult is the test of wills. Strong personalities with strong opinions can equal some feisty fireworks. At our age, flexibility is not so easy.

I'd be disingenuous to tell you all was rosy.

Our marriage faced a few hurdles, particularly the first year. "BACK OFF" was code to warn the other our limit was reached. The code word got quite a workout that first year.

Now, with nearly twenty years under our belt, I can testify, Richard truly has loved me like no man has ever loved me. He loves me just the way I am: strange, quirky, and all. Bless his heart. It's how we roll.

"BACK OFF" is rarely used anymore.

Wedding Gift

On the heels of our honeymoon, a cynical salutation repeated its threat on every voicemail we had. "Congratulations on your marriage and happy birthday. Oh, by the way, you owe me money. Those crypts are worth thousands more than you said."

Arrogantly the familiar voice warns, "pay me or I'll see you in court."

The slithering snake has returned!

"How dare him! He thinks because I got married there is money!" To put it ever-so-kindly I'm mad! Seething, spittin' MAD! Ready to unleash rusty backhanded maneuvers, that kind of mad.

The calm groom inquires of his sizzlin' hot bride, "Talk about skeletons in the closet. Anything else you've neglected to tell me?"

Our honeymoon is spoiled by an ex.

"Looks like we have a project. Pull out all the docs." Richard gives directives. "Let's see what the documents say. Bet it's not what you think."

The smallest of details does not escape this heavenly gift. Layers I never knew existed unfold as Richard's expertise, and wisdom, come to light.

After exploring the dusty divorce decree, Richard says, "As painful as it is Reneé, you owe him money."

"NO! I owe half. Everything was split in half!"

"According to this paragraph, the twelve-hundred-dollar escrow belongs to him. As far as the mausoleum crypts are concerned, you both were responsible to get them sold. Why does he think selling the crypts was all your responsibility?"

"Based on the conversation in the lawyer's office, it was assigned to me. Do you recall when Bobbi passed, I tried to sell them to you? For months, a sign was posted on the mirror advertising the cemetery plots."

"I recall."

Idea flash! "I'll run an ad in the local newspaper with his phone number. 'Crypts for two, make offer. Must sell!' I'm all over it."

"You go, girl." Richard shakes his head in agreement.

His tenacious bride refuses to pay three hundred dollars an hour for a stinkin' lawyer.

"Reneé, you're a *can-do* woman. Represent yourself." Richard's words reinforce my decision.

We are a couple of unicorns.

We review documents and strategize. Truth be told, I think I'm brighter than I really am. Really, I'm just bold and courageous. Hope it doesn't ruin me.

God brings clients and friends to apprise me how to navigate the legal system. Plus, firsthand experience helps. Prepared, armed with knowledge and prayer.

Court day arrives.

Let there be no mistake, Court is serious business. "Dress for success," they say. What does a bride-turned snake slayer wear into battle? Confident professional choices. Kick-a$$ cowgirl boots, yes, that's what one wears along with a white broomstick skirt and a turquoise top. Now add a silver concha leather belt to the ensemble. Confident. Dressed to kill. Armed. Ready for battle!

"Come to court with me, Richard."

"Nope, you got it handled. Walk in as if you own the place. You'll be just fine, Luv."

Slightly nervous, Snake Slayer flies out the door.

Driving to the courthouse, the Holy Spirit warns, *"Watch your back."*

Snake Slayer sits with her back to the courtroom walls, facing the isle to avert surprises. Within minutes of settling into a seat, the serpent slithers down the aisle, accompanied by a young dapper hotshot lawyer strutting a pressed gray Armani suit.

Smug intimidation fills the room.

Why is Ben here? I question. *He lives in Tennessee. Court was between his attorney and me.* That's how much I know. Huh! No one warned me of this possibility.

Hidden behind dark shady glasses, the snake slides upon the stand. Quite a sight to watch. Irrelevant questions are asked of Ben. Seemed to me like his attorney was chasing his own tail.

Mr. Hotshot makes a nasty comment about the five-year delay of the crypt ad posted two weeks prior to court.

Pointless questions continue, "Ben, how much are those crypts valued today?

"Eight thousand dollars."

"No further questions."

"Ms. Budde, please take the stand." None of that, "Do you swear to tell the truth?" with your "hand on the Bible" business. Mr. Hotshot politely asks a few questions about real estate transactions.

An impressive show of words orchestrated to intimidate. It'll take more than a slick tongue to intimidate me. God's warning comes to mind. I sense a trap in the making.

"Ms. Budde, what is ---- in real estate?"

Serpent Slayer shrugs, "I wouldn't know the answer to your question. I do hair, not real estate."

Hotshot strategizes his intimidation tactic, elevates his voice, and presents the same question with a slightly different twist.

I'm not fooled by his tomfoolery of words.

The judge smacks down Hotshot's coercing nonsense with a stern warning! His trap has gone awry. He mistakenly assumed the defendant would be fragile and burst into tears under his manipulative spell.

Instead, razor focused, I repeat, "Real estate is not my area of expertise. I do not know the answer to your question."

Lamebrain, is that the best you can do?

"You may step down, Ms. Budde."

Now it's *my* turn to ask questions, pertinent ones. Authority rises. The Slayer throws a fiery dart.

"Mr. Thomas, is there any provision within this divorce decree that excludes you from performing your obligation due to health or state in which you reside?"

"No."

Sizzle!

"Mr. Thomas, would you please read aloud paragraph two on page ten."

This is a game changer!

The anticipated gotcha moment is interrupted by the judge's insistence to read the document for herself. Darn! Neither Ben nor his lawyer know what she's about to feast her eyes upon.

Silently she read the explosive piece, "*Both parties* shall do their best to see the cemetery plots are sold."

KABOOM! Fiery darts strike. SIZZLE. Burnt to an ash heap.

The kill shot comes undetected. The plaintiffs have no idea what just slapped them hard!

Torched by a wickedly good Snake Slayer. Touché!

"Mr. Thomas, regarding the ad, did you receive any phone calls for the mausoleum crypts?"

"No."

"Could it be, Mr. Thomas, that selling used crypts is like buying a dead horse?! No one wants them." The flame thrower smokes the well-rehearsed line!

Thrilled is an understatement! To incorporate that humorous play on words delights my soul.

Just try to restrain JOY. Go ahead, try. You can't. Snake Slayer turns away and grins ear to ear.

(FYI: crypts are not reusable. That's beside the point.)

Assuredly, the gotcha trap continues. Like leading a horse to water, only this horse *will* drink. He'll have no choice. Nearly giddy about the take down, yet outwardly restrained.

"Mr. Thomas, what did *you* do to see the crypts were sold?"

"Nothing."

KABOOM!!! FLAMES ERUPT! Drop the mic!!!

Silence sizzles the snake's remains. Not to gloat, too much anyway, Snake Slayer turns her back, punching the air!! *YES! YES! YES!* Jubilant fireworks explode!

I smoked him again! I just proved Ben guilty for the very matter he's suing me for. I'M STOKED!!

The ash heap has no idea what just smoked his case, as he never read the document. Too bad.

"No further questions, your honor."

Just as Richard discovered, I had to pay the escrow balance. However, on the crypts count, I am not held liable.

The judge and Ben's lawyer engage in a brief discussion regarding fees, dates, etcetera. That seemed to wrap up court. Not so fast.

Mr. Hotshot sends the Slain One into the corner to lick his wounds. The lawyer extends his hand in a conciliatory gesture. In a southern drawl uncommon here in the west, "Ms. Budde, never in my ten years of practicing law, have I experienced anything quite the likes of you. If only you had answered my questions."

The Victorious One cordially obliges his handshake, thinking, *oh you mean the trap questions?* Hahahaha.

"Mr. Hotshot, I came to kick a$$. And I just did."

Buried in a heap, the man on fire smolders.

Without boring you with messy details and such, the Slain One is awarded only one hundred sixty-eight dollars of the over three-thousand-dollar attorney fees.

Jubilation explodes on so many levels. Sweet vindication!!

In retrospect, lots of credit goes to the Slain One. His shenanigans kick-started Richard's and my marriage. A wedding gift of sorts. Court preparation catapulted the bride and groom's relationship into Team We. What a great gift! Unicorns unified!

Not to be redundant but, "Vindication is mine; I will repay says the Lord."

After the dust settled, I gifted Ben the crypts, to stomp out further shenanigans.

A tough lesson to be had: Don't mess with a Snake Slayer!

Stephen Ministries

Time is required for newlyweds to find their groove. Richard wants to be involved in church outreach. His wife is hesitant; she wants to concentrate on their marriage. Don't get me wrong, if a year of matrimonial bliss was under our belt, I might be more receptive. Stephen Ministries requires a weekly commitment of several hours. The powers that be don't allow spousal participation; we've checked. We remain stuck, unmovable. The untouched application remains amongst paperwork in my back seat.

On the way home from church, the discussion of the unsettled topic continues.

My trusty little Corolla whips into the secluded greenbelt parking lot. Iris doesn't begin to compare to Richard's canary Corvette, but her stick on the floor enables her to twirl in place like a hot rod, and she can plow through a wicked snowstorm, unlike those garage beauties when the weather turns ugly. Sure do miss that old car.

Back to our unresolved issue. Hand in hand we meander along the tree-lined greenbelt, cultivating the art of persuasion. The ministry startup date breathes heavily down our backs.

Richard has never participated in any type of ministry. This was his hot pursuit before "we" came along.

Approaching a park beach, Mr. Budde invites his bride, "have a seat, Luv."

An Indian summer grants a glorious backdrop. "We both must agree upon whatever we do." Richard's passion shines to persuade. "It enables me to change a life."

Hard to resist a man of passion. Truly, a rare find.

The conflict is not over ministry but timing. As newlyweds we were shot out of a canon by an ex.

"We should invest in our marriage. Since I work a couple of evenings a week and if you're gone two to three nights, where is time for us?" I state my cause. "If teamwork was allowed, this would be an easy decision. But it's not."

Disagreement is futile. We agree to pray. "Lord, help us. Make it crystal clear what we're to do." We leave the unresolved situation with God on the park bench.

Afternoon temperatures begin to broil. Into Iris we jump, crack the windows, turn on the air conditioner, and briskly dart away.

Richard's overly sensitive sniffer inhales, "Can you get a whiff of the pleasant fall breeze?"

Sweet aromas are his Bride's dim memory.

Suddenly a strong gust of wind blows violently about inside the car. Papers toss in a whirlwind. *Whoosh!* An escapee flutters out the narrowly cracked window! To avoid further evacuation, I quickly crank up the windows.

After we arrived home and sorted through the disheveled mess, that we realize the only missing paper is the Stephen Ministries application.

Slap us silly! The dumbfounded bride and groom froze in place.

Go Ahead, Mock Me

"Don't be ridiculous! Why do you bother God?" Richard scorns, "He doesn't care about such trivial nonsense."

I choose to pay no attention to his ridiculing ways. So, we believe differently. Makes for some interesting conversations!

Call me silly or strange, no matter where I go or how congested parking is, I expect God to provide a front parking space. It's true. Without fail I drive right to a front spot.

Richard doesn't believe me either. I'm used to it.

Take our trip to the zoo, for example. We drive past hundreds of cars lined up for blocks before entering the zoo's packed lot. I refuse to settle for a spot along the way.

Snidely, Richard comments, "Why do you waste time praying for a parking place?"

"I don't anymore. I just go to the front."

"You won't get one today."

It's hard to shake that man's disbelief.

"I always drive right to it. The spot waits for me. You should know this by now. Babe, I'll drop you off to meet the family and be right back after I park."

"Sure, you will," he hurls a sarcastic remark for the journey.

Sight for sore eyes is dropped off at the curb. He's certain, not to expect me until nightfall.

"You should have packed a lunch," shouts the skeptic.

This'll be fun. Ready to prove my point, Iris whips around the corner, steps from the zoo's front entry takes her awaited space. Hardly a minute passes before the scorned one proudly sneaks up on the skeptic.

I didn't have to slap 'em silly. The evidence speaks for itself.

The flabbergasted turn their heads, pick their jaws up from the sidewalk, and ask, "How did you do that?"

"I keep telling you. If you can't believe God for a parking place, how can you believe Him for healing a headache or cancer?"

Guess who's now a big believer in petitioning God for the smallest of needs? No longer do I endure the constant ridicule or mocking for wasting God's time for the insignificant.

Note to self: Believing God for small stuff is REALLY BIG!

Nighttime Entertainment

My shoes are ready to blow off! My new husband and I have never talked about this subject. It just never came up. The truth is, I dream prophetically.

You might wonder how I know the difference between prophetic and ordinary dreams? If the dream is recalled in detail and cannot be shaken from my thoughts, it's prophetic. Seldom is it understood. If it's an ordinary dream I barely recall it, if at all.

Friday is date night. Last night's dream will make for a delicious side dish or main entree.

Dinner has arrived at our table. No longer can I hold onto my blessed shoes. I have words!

"Richard, last night, I had a dream. It was troubling."

"Okay," tilting his head and shrugging his shoulder in curiosity. "Let's talk about it."

Anxious to keep my shoes from catching fire, I begin, "The dream was so real. Bobbi was only presumed dead. You weren't home when she knocked at the door. Frantic, I wasn't sure what to do. Invite her in? Do I share you, apologize, and explain our recent marriage? Or leave and return her back to you? I was torn. It was really upsetting."

Put off by the preposterous dream, Richard adamantly insists, "Bobbi is not coming home. She is dead and will never return."

"I know that, Richard. You don't understand. I wouldn't recall the dream if there wasn't something to it."

"We'll just call your dream, nighttime entertainment."

"It's more than that!" I insist.

"No, there is nothing to it. Let's drop it," Richard insists.

The conversation went ice cold.

No resolution followed. I just can't shake the dream. There's something prophetic about it. What, I don't know, but I'm determined to figure it out.

Passionate kisses are replaced with a peck. Puzzle pieces begin to fit together and make sense.

Every Friday I have asked the question, "What did you do today?"

Without fail, Richard's response was identical, "Oh, I dropped by the cemetery during lunch hour."

Bobbi's graveside is Richard's Friday afternoon ritual. I quit asking. I know. The peck spoke volumes. No woman can compete with a dead woman for the love of a man. There is no good solution in sight.

In solitude, tears of grief flow.

If you want a picture of a great marriage which weathered storms and flourish, it was Richard and Bobbi's. I knew that. We knew each other over seventeen years. Such respect. Richard and Bobbi were kind to one another. They never spoke poorly of one another. It was obvious, great respect wove their marriage together.

We silently limp our way through the first year. It is hard to process the tug-of-war I feel. A week lapses between daggers. The dream has prepared me for my new reality.

I share my husband with a dead woman.

Every week I cry out, "God, what do I do?" No answers, only silence. Divine intervention brought us together. Don't assume that translates into easy.

Remarriage is difficult. Older couples are ingrained in kid's lives, family traditions, food choices, habits such as toilet lids or how to squeeze the toothpaste and other matters of significance. If anyone tells you it's easy, they lie.

Ten months since the troubling dream…

Five p.m. the garage door opens. My Friday date has arrived. Richard calls out with a disconcerting tone, "Reneé." A sense of urgency carries throughout the house. "Reneé, I've got to talk with you."

With a gentle squeeze to my hand, Richard leads me to the sofa. "Please, sit down."

This pre-date meeting is highly unconventional. *Hmmm.*

His eyes turn weepy. His voice cracks. "I am so sorry."

Confused by his unexpected apology. "For what?"

"I was at Bobbi's grave today when the Spirit of the Lord spoke to me. *'You told Reneé you would forsake all others. That includes living and the dead.'* I am so sorry. If our marriage is to soar, I must let Bobbi go. Please forgive me."

Instantly, both hands cupped my lips. Richard's head falls into my lap. Sobs drench hearts and lap.

Still all these years later, God's intervention overwhelms me.

It took months for the dream to become crystal clear. Just as the dream suggested, "I shared Richard with Bobbi."

The Park

Rollerblades fit snug as a glove. Trunk lid slides down; the man is off! Richard loves blading the park during lunch. A welcome reprieve from the cubical life of an engineer. See the small farm nestled next door? Hens cackle. Horses bask on the warm earthen floor. Ducks squawk and splash to protect their domain. Now there's a whole lot of muddly whompin' going on in the barnyard.

Barnyard sounds and aromas are not everyone's forte. Some find it therapeutic. Others not so much, particularly if in close proximity.

Richard greets familiar faces as he circles the park's mile track. It's not often a white-haired guy struts his stuff on rollerblades without breaking a sweat. No doubt, bystanders want his autograph. Even the kids admire his agility. You might think I'm a little braggadocious, but I've seen it firsthand.

Richard sails past the playground, noticing a disheveled man slouched on the park bench. *Whish*!

An inner voice quietly says, ***"Stop and talk to that guy."***

He sloughs off the voice with, "don't bother me. Don't you know, I'm on my lunch hour?"

Wheels whiz past. Richard's three-mile routine requires time. Limited time. He circles the pond again, glides upon the fella a second time. *Avoid eye contact; pay no attention to the man sitting on the bench,* he tells himself.

Engineer types seem to struggle with flexibility. Once the plan is in motion, there is no deviation. If they shift midstream, their mojo is forever altered! It's tragic really.

On the third lap, the stranger remains seated on the park bench.

The voice gets louder, *"Stop and talk to the man!"*

Richard turns a deaf ear. *Whoosh!* Those blades accelerate past the dreaded man on the bench!

"HEY!" The guy yells at Richard. "Come back and talk to me!"

Now if that doesn't yank your stubborn chain I don't know what will! (So, you think you're too busy, huh?)

Can't you see God belly laugh and proclaim, **GOTCHA**!?

Slap Mr. Budde straight! The staunch engineer screeches to a halt, turns around, and plops alongside the stranger sitting on the park bench.

The man's arms are all marred with slashes. He wanted to talk to someone. Not just anyone. He needed my husband. A very personal conversation was initiated.

After much discussion Richard asked, "May I pray for you?"

The stranger obliges with a nod.

On that park bench, two men, strangers no more, pray. Oppression lifts. Hope replenished. Countenance transformed. Hugs exchanged. Lives changed. A day of blading divinely interrupted on a park bench.

Imagine

Sleepless nights invade the life of a menopausal woman. Life is turned upside down, inside out and hot, hot, hot!

Ding, ding, ding, the brainchild is awakened. Endless hot flashes disturb her sleep. It's two thirty in the morning! Again.

"Lord, what does one do in the middle of the night when one cannot sleep?"

Quickly a response follows, *"Write that book you always talked about."*

"Now, Lord, poetry and church productions are my gig, not books. I'm hardly qualified to write a book. You know I'm special."

This girl wears the badge proudly. Whatever you do, do it well. In my youth my kind was referred to as special ed. Then poof! Being special is no longer politically correct, I guess. Today, all that "specialness" is labeled dyslexia. What's so special about dyslexia? Nothing. Makes one think they are handicapped or something.

Back to… "Me write a book? Really? Lord, do you realize what you're asking?"

Deafening silence follows. He lets me stew.

Okay. OKAY. God doesn't argue. He makes his point and leaves it up to me. He's gracious. And I try to remain flexible. It's how I roll.

A coffee-table book would be a nice family heirloom. Sure, writing will give me something to do in the middle of the night. No big deal. Famous last words.

Several chapters later, my sister visits from California. "Hey Denise, would you look over these stories? See if the facts are as you recall them."

"Sure, should I correct it as well?" She can't help herself. It's what teachers do.

I deem it a waste of time, as it's way too early, but if that's what it takes for her to read it, "Why not?"

Before leaving town, Denise hands over the manuscript drenched in red. "Sorry, I didn't finish. Got into the story and set down the pen. Again, I'm sorry."

Now that may not sound complimentary to you, but the fact she laid the red pen down spoke volumes.

How about another viewpoint?

"Richard, I'd like you to read this chapter. Give me your honest feedback." He has an astute eye and taste, not to mention he's my most honest fan.

"Wow! This is really good."

"Will you read another chapter on our trip?"

"Certainly, I'd love to."

Richard reads. I drive. Pages stop turning. Curiosity kicks in.

"What did you think?"

Silence.

"Richard, what did you think?"

His silence is deafening. *He's not certain how to tell me it's no good.* Buttercup sucks it up to ask in a different tone. "Richard, what do you think?"

I glance over and there he sits in a puddle.

"Never mind."

The chatterbox spills the beans of the project underway to all who enter the salon, garnished with Denise and Richard's reactions. Over and over, encouraging words propel me to consider the book beyond the coffee table version.

Diana's words strike a profound chord, "It could be greater than you think, ask, or imagine." Now, she and I never discuss things of God, so when she quoted Ephesians 3:20 almost word for word, it blew me away!

I'm blessed to be in the *best* profession *ever*! Not only do I make people look and feel incredible, but the trickle effect of relationships is beyond fulfilling. Who would have thunk this author's salon chair would be the hub for an unskilled writer?

A nudge from above comes as Melissa sits in my chair. *"Ask if she'll read your manuscript."* I had no idea Melissa had a literary degree. Slap me stunned.

"I planned to stop by the library on my way home for something to read." This simple nudge transitions into Melissa filling the position of editor. Pushing through chewed fingernails, hair loss, and multiple rewrites, plus a few therapy sessions, Melissa molds me into a bona fide author. Not an easy undertaking for either of us.

"Reneé, how did you acquire the mare?"

Annoyed by Melissa's push to introduce the story beyond the one I wanted to tell. "What difference does that make?"

"Your reader wants to know."

Hmmm, not happy, but I write it. Melissa is thrilled; me not so much. Something is wrong, but what? Determined to figure it out, I feel the nudge again when an English teacher sits in my chair for a haircut.

"Patrice, would you look at my manuscript. Tell me what you think?"

"Sure, Reneé, I'd be happy to."

A few weeks later Patrice tells me, "If I didn't know you, I would have put the manuscript down. It wasn't until chapter three that you flourish."

"Why? What was wrong?" I ask, hoping for specifics as this was the very content I struggled with.

"I felt I was reading a dictionary, just the facts. Once you connect to your horse, it all changed."

BINGO!!

"Oh, thank you, Patrice. You have been incredibly helpful."

Now to make the changes.

Further resistance happens. The editor attempts to persuade me to omit the "religious" chapter. Swords are drawn, ready to fight to the chapter's death. I believe "Protection" to be critical to the storyline.

"Lord, 'Protection' will serve no purpose if readers put *Cody* book down. What should I do?"

"Warn people," the Spirit of God directs.

What a great idea, "Thanks, Lord!"

Another client says, "I'll proof your book when you're done, if you like." At nearly ninety-years young, Phyl's proofreading went back to generals in World War II. Such a gift.

Who would have guessed my daughter's higher education would produce *Cody*'s beautiful cover design? Don't you worry, she was paid handsomely.

After selling out the first edition, God nudged me to revise and improve the entire manuscript. Seems so brutal to rewrite the *entire* manuscript. God knew I was not happy with His request.

Bits 'n pieces will do the special one decides.

Storytelling is easy, wordsmithing, well, not so much. To rewrite *Cody* means work, lots of work! To dig in and say, "I'll NEVER" quickly backfires. Halfway through the edit my computer starts to smoke! Firefighters are needed on the scene to extinguish flames and give mouth to mouth resuscitation to the author in heart failure.

No doubt, God laughed.

Thank the Geek Squad for rescuing the dying device. Spared the uncomfortable mouth-to-mouth resuscitation.

Oh, glorious day! Stoked I am! *Cody* is complete! Confetti erupts! Bring out the bubbly!

Celebration abruptly halts as I open the file and find two, that's right TWO *Cody* books!

"OH, NOOO!! How can this be?"

Evidently fingers dabbled in both manuscripts! Neither were complete! Guess what that means? That's right, a *Cody* book rewrite in its entirety! The very thing the defiant one announced she'd NEVER do. FINE! Just fine!

Bertha

Ring! Ring! "Hello."

"Hi, Hun, I need a favor."

"Sure, Luv, what do you need?"

"When you're out today, will you pick up some flowers? They are for another woman," he nonchalantly adds. "A small bouquet, nothing big. She's a small-framed lady. I'll explain later. I love you Mrs. Budde. See you tonight!"

Click.

Now, you might say, "How could you let flowers for another woman slide by without interrogation?"

"I know my man. I trust him. Now, I've got things to do, like go buy flowers, not answer to you."

Dinner guests are coming tonight, so I'll arrange a bouquet for the table as well. The hunt is on. In front of the flower case I stand, pondering, undecided. Hmmm.

"Oh, Lord, it's not what I enjoy. You know this lady's favorite flower. Help. Which flowers should I choose?"

Finally, my eyes zero in on winter white roses. Ding. Ding. Ding. White roses it is!

Great care is taken to create a tiny arrangement. Of course, my curiosity is stirred, but I'm not worried. Some, like yourself, might think I'm naïve, but I've known this charming man for many years.

Like clockwork, at five p.m. through the kitchen door my husband bounds. Handsome as always. We embrace with warm hugs and kisses and a little rubbing too. A state of frequent occurrence here at the Budde house. We like it.

Days of pecks are gone. Woot! Woot!

"Hi, Luv. I love you so much, you are such a fabulous wife!" The kisses continue and continue ….

Oh stop!

Excited to show off my floral masterpiece, the rubbing and smouching session must end.

"Here, babe, follow me." I lead Richard down the hallway, switch on the light and behold, a simple collection of foliage and baby's breath peaks from beneath three white rose buds in a small crystal vase.

Richard gasps. Tears swell. He's overcome. Truly, the arrangement's simplicity is nice, but not worthy of this reaction.

Stunned, Richard says, "Sitting at my desk this afternoon I was thinking, winter white roses is what I want for this little lady. And look, you did just that! But I never told you!"

I smile. That's what God does. Curiosity awaits! "Now that you're home, do tell." The readers want to know too.

"I was driving down Sheridan Boulevard this morning and passed by an elderly hunched-over woman walking down the street. I see her frequently. This morning, the Spirit of God spoke to me: *'Help this lady.'* I thought I'd give her flowers."

"Richard, flowers won't help her. If you are to help, she needs more than flowers."

"I thought I'd enclose some cash in a card. But I want to give her flowers too."

A sign of approval transfers through our gaze.

Cash is the right thing to do.

"They are perfect! I didn't want anything too large, as she struggles to walk. I'll take the bouquet in the morning."

"How do you know she'll be there?"

"Oh, she'll be there."

Our dinner guests arrive. Intriguing discussion transpires over the strange occurrences of the day. It was too much to bear for the curious ones. They'd have to wait an entire week before knowing the outcome. I know. I know.

The next morning. Six a.m. Time to go. Extra time is allotted for flower delivery. Twenty minutes later, Richard spots her. He pulls over, grabs the card and flowers, and chases after the mystery woman.

She hears a runner fast approaching and shuffles off the path to allow him access.

"Ma'am, Ma'am!" Richard calls out.

The small frail frame slowly turns toward Mr. Budde. He senses her concern of a stranger's approach and warmly extends the small bouquet of flowers toward her.

"These are for you."

Abruptly the little lady pulls away from his gesture and skeptically asks, "Why?"

"God told me to give them to you."

The old woman abruptly grabs the flowers from Richard's hand and vigorously thrusts the bouquet to her breast.

Her feeble hand graciously extends toward Richard as she politely responds, "My name is Bertha."

Clothed in a warm smile, Richard extends his hand. "It's a pleasure to meet you, Bertha, my name is—"

"You are Richard," Bertha interrupts his salutation. "I've been praying for you."

Slap us speechless!

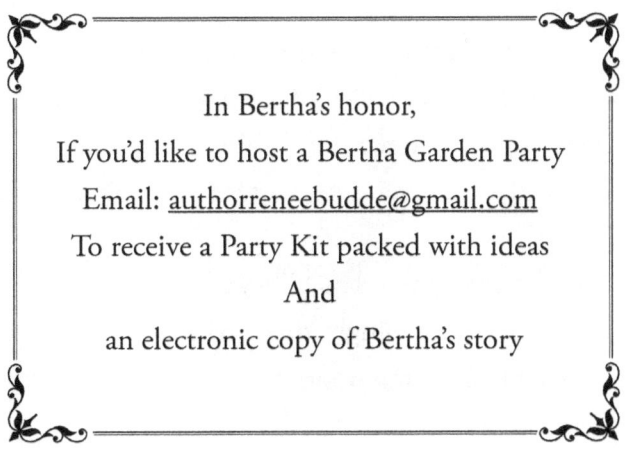

In Bertha's honor,
If you'd like to host a Bertha Garden Party
Email: authorreneebudde@gmail.com
To receive a Party Kit packed with ideas
And
an electronic copy of Bertha's story

No Good Deed

Ever lived through a flood? If so, you know the destruction. Unimaginable. Overwhelming. Words are hardly adequate to describe the overwhelming debris.

September 2013 a five-hundred-year flood hit Lyons, a charming town in Colorado's foothills. Lyons Park was a favorite spot for my riding partner and I to horseback ride. So when flood waters took out our favorite community, I was compelled, *what can I do to make an impact?*

Filled with wild and crazy ideas. A logical one comes to light. Provide Thanksgiving dinner for the entire community! Perfect. Willing clients jump on board.

Now look for a spot to host the dinner. Either a church or community center will suffice. That's the plan. Robert Burns knew what he was talking about in his 1786 poem: "The best laid plans of mice and men. They often go awry."

Over several weeks, phone calls in search of a viable location to host dinner were made. No place will allow us to use their facility.

What does a disappointed girl do? Trade hospitality for cleanup. That's what a girl does. Rope in the Mister and his mighty dump truck too.

FEMA landed a spot I could not. They fed the distraught community on Thanksgiving Day. Surprisingly, they invited us. Unlike many Lyons residents, we live far from the impacted area and have a stove, power, and operational house.

Sunrise, Friday after Thanksgiving, we pull up with a dump truck and trailer to meet up with fellow volunteers.

Fascinating to watch FEMA's fine-oiled machine up close. Volunteers congregate on West Main Street at the local church, awaiting FEMA's directives.

Each team member receives an identifying VOLUNTEER T-shirt to wear.

Standing in line for our assignment, we got educated. FEMA is not a free meal ticket. Nor does FEMA do all the cleanup. The town MUST match the hours invested. More "credit value" is given for our dump truck and trailer than labor alone.

Larry, a local retiree, and two young professional transplants wearing "Frozen Dead Man Festival" T-shirts made up our team of volunteers. Sounds peculiar, I know, but such a thing actually exists. Both the frozen dead guy and the annual festival. The fellas thought it was a gag. Locals know better. This is Colorado. Need I say more?

The FEMA coordinator directs Larry: "Go to the home tucked down the steep drive off the highway. Clean up the debris in the yard. Use the roll-offs in the center of town to dump the debris. Then report back for your next assignment."

Young bucks hop in the truck, and we follow Larry to the house described.

Gawking, through the apocalyptic mine field. Gnarly uprooted trees lay everywhere. Unrecognizable massive balls of wreckage hang from hillsides. Portions of tires or license plates stick out. Those balls were vehicles. Homes cut in half, as if for a movie, furniture and wallpaper remain intact. Unimaginable.

"Stop! That's one of the churches I'd called when looking for a spot to host Thanksgiving dinner."

Richard pulls the caravan into the unscathed parking lot.

Curious, I jump out and run inside.

Yellow caution tape and signs everywhere. Watch your step. The floor is missing, and a river runs through the sanctuary.

Pastor can't help notice my stunned expression and says, "the river will be redirected."

I'm sickened by the devastation.

But they're killin' the cleanup!

No wonder they can't host dinner. Snap, snap, snap, the historian snaps a ton of photos. Unfortunately, the snapshots floated away in the cloud.

Down the driveway in low gear we crawl toward our destination, mesmerized by unbelievable sights. The river certainly left its mark. Richard dodges huge boulders, river rocks, and uprooted monster trees. The front yard is consumed with flood debris, yet a sapling protected by a three-foot-high swirl of dirt rises in the midst. Strange.

Curiously we explore the abandoned home. In some respects, it looks untouched. In others, the water had its way.

Hear tell, the powers that be won't allow rebuilding along the river's edge. Tragically understandable.

We each slip on leather gloves to pitch everything in our path into the convoy. Young bucks are fast.

Trailers and dump trucks are loaded to the max.

Mr. Budde sent the Mrs. with directives to slow down traffic on the highway so the convoy could safely pop up, blindly enter from the abyss, and make a sharp turn, all without incident.

Sounds dangerous, right?

Mr. Budde follows up with, "wear this reflective vest and set these safety cones on the roadside."

The vested babe hikes up the steep drive, marks the entry with cones, and stands on the highway's edge, arms flailing.

Drivers pay no mind to the glowing woman in fluorescent stripes. *This'll never do.*

The debris train chugs up the hidden drive.

Courage propels the glowing one toward the highway's center to stop traffic in both directions.

Travelers should be aware of commotion and detours since the cleanup began. Braveheart waves her arms like Mama did when giving us the business. Only this mama is on steroids.

Receiving NO cooperation, I get creative. An effective technique used in the classroom and at home by fourth-grade teacher Mama was the LOOK.

Well, I whip it out, with a bona fide yell: *"YOU BOYS ARE IN TROUBLE!!!* SLOW DOWN!!"

Don't let this curly top fool you. Mama taught me well.

No doubt, drivers recognize the LOOK. A trucker almost runs me over, for cryin' out loud! I'm a big girl in plain sight, with a safety vest! Truly, I am sweating it as the semi's brakes screech to a halt. Could he not see me!? How often does one see a glowing babe smack in the middle of a highway?

I want to slap that trucker, hurt him just a little. Okay, a lot. Instead, I halt the other side of oncoming traffic, grab the cones, and jump inside the moving caravan, as it slowly makes a U-turn wide enough for a freight train before roaring off. Mission accomplished! That sure was fun.

Our next assignment: A pile of rubbish needs to be picked up in front of a resident's home.

Heaps are shoveled into the trailer. The pile is nearly clear when the intoxicated neighbor decides he should manage our project. Bad choice on his part.

"Don't sweep the nails like that," he tells us.

Silence falls. Well-behaved volunteers have no response to the drunkard's misguided directives. However, the feisty one cannot hold her tongue. "If you think you can do a better job, grab a broom and show us how it's done!" After all, I am my mother's daughter and don't tolerate that kind of nonsense. He's messin' with the wrong girl!

Is he blind? Our T-shirts are marked VOLUNTEER in big bold letters.

Potty mouth spews lude suggestions and derogatory names at the feisty one.

Ooh, my mad juices rev up. *"DON'T TALK TO ME LIKE THAT!"* Tempted to inflict some serious damage with a stiff right swing when her knight-in-shining-armor intercepts.

The bibbed overall knight furiously high-hurdles the heap and roars upon the drunk and lets him have it! "NOBODY TALKS TO MY WIFE LIKE THAT AND GETS AWAY WITH IT!"

"Go ahead, old man," the obnoxious drunk challenges.

Hair on fire, the knight spouts back, "I'm going to knock your lights out!" And wallops him good.

Not wanting to be left out of a rip-roarin' good time, the two bucks join the slug fest.

"STOP!" the feisty one shouts. "Let's get out of here before we all get hauled off to the pokey."

Richard and I jump into the truck and shout, "Come on boys, leave him be."

The fellas come a runnin' and jump into the moving truck. Excited, they proclaim, "You should write a book!"

"No good deed goes unpunished," Mr. Budde mutters as Mrs. Budde hands the boys an autographed copy of *Cody Life Lessons Inspired By My Spirited Mare.*

Did we stay out of jail or was the drunk spared a serious beating because of Bertha's prayers? Maybe both.

God Bless Bertha.

The Ladder

If you could embody anyone's super power, whose would it be? Today, Michelangelo's is mine. My perfectionist husband has taken the bathroom project to completion's edge.

"Today, I'm painting the ceiling." Michelangelo announces.

The perfectionist responds, "I'll get it, luv."

"No, no, no," the stubborn impersonator insists. "You've done so much. Let me finish."

"I wish you wouldn't."

It's hard to satisfy his discriminating taste. Transformation of Richard's home into *our* home has been a process. The main bathroom hosts an oversized garden tub in lieu of a shower.

What contractor builds a main suite bathroom without a shower? Yes, he should have his license revoked.

There is no room for both. Instead of ripping out the tub to make way for a shower, we simply add *two* shower heads to make a tub/shower combo (winky, winky). Large travertine spa tiles replace cheesy four-inch contractor tiles. AH.

Now for the ceiling.

"Reneé, I wish you'd leave the painting for me."

"It won't take long. I insist. Let me finish it."

The simple word, "NO" grates as fingernails on a chalkboard! Two peas in a pod we are.

"You're going to fall!" Mr. Budde proclaims.

Sometimes he makes me so mad, I could slap him! "Richard, get out of here. I am not going to fall!"

Finally, the garage door closes behind him. "Fine. Just fine."

Driven by an afterthought, the menacing Mister returns. "I better cover the tub for your protection." Unrelenting, the man of safety lays out all the appropriate tools to "soften the blow."

"You'll need a phone nearby," Richard emphatically insists as he covers the tub with a stiff sheet of plywood backed with carpet to protect the tub's surface.

"This will keep from scratching the tub on impact."

Isn't he considerate?

"Stop worrying!" Deliverance can't come soon enough. "I've never fallen off a ladder. Get out of here."

He won't let it go. "Where's your phone?"

Seasoned with a sneer of sarcasm, I pat the cell nestled securely in my upper pocket, "It's right here."

"I wouldn't put it there. It'll break when you fall."

God's Word says, you can have what you say. It's not limited to only the good stuff.

Michelangelo slams the house phone on the countertop, aims the paintbrush towards Mister's eye and snaps, "Are you pleased now? Leave before I do something I'll regret."

FINALLY, the Mister leaves.

Let the makeover begin. Color of spa splashes sterile white walls. No special license needed to stroke a paintbrush. If you don't like it, change it. It's only paint for crying out loud.

Now I'll admit, ceilings are harder. Ask Michelangelo. Not all painters are hardbodies capable of stretching above their head and shoulders to create a masterpiece.

Suck it up girlfriend. You asked for it.

In comparison to today's oversized bathroom suites, ours is a bit snug. Barely room for a six-foot ladder much less a voluptuous painter flicking her cape.

Did I mention Richard placed sheets of cardboard on the floor? Pretty foreign idea. Hear tell, it's all about safety. According to his behavior this morning, my safety is paramount.

Stepladder workouts make calves look sexy, a lovely side benefit. The giddy impersonator ascends up the ladder rungs.

Tip for marriage survival: incorporate knowledge taught by meticulous spouse. Define the line perfectly. Work the brush as taught.

The Budde philosophy proudly flows: "mediocrity is lame." We can't help ourselves.

Not to brag, but I have outdone my bad self with such a straight line. Michelangelo would be proud. For sure the perfectionist will be. A little gloat never hurt.

Bravely the impersonator inches her way toward the tippy top of Sistine Chapel's ceiling. Whew, those additional eight feet sure bring on some intense hot flashes!

Flippin' painter capes are highly overrated.

"AH, now that's cooler." Naked beats hot 'n' sticky.

Fresh paint in hand, calisthenics commence. Snarky sarcasm twirls the rotisserie skewer, "When you fall, you'll need a phone."

I wish Richard had never implied such a disaster. Unable to shake his worrisome words, a prayer seems to be appropriate.

"Lord, protect me."

Richard's troubling comments continue to haunt me as I proceed to paint the chapel's skylight shaft.

"Okay, okay!"

Down the ladder the testy impersonator descends. Retrieves her cape amongst other paraphernalia of the woven type and moves the communicator device to the tub's edge. Just in case a fall does happen, a phone should be readily accessible.

A voluptuous Michelangelo lying on the floor would be a ghastly sight not easily unseen, should a bare-naked painter fall.

Cause for some disagreement over this point of the story could be had, but I'm telling the story, and it was bad! This is what really happened. After all, I am the only eyewitness here.

Remember that floor protection under the ladder?
Well, cockeyed it became.
Protective covering is the blame
for a lop-eared ladder, which bore no shame.

I saw it just as plain as day coming my way.
Yet still I climb toward the tippy top.
Paint in hand situated on the wobbly stand.

This pretty sight will not end well, I can tell.
Arms outstretched flail
as the dancing ladder takes an awful spill.

Waffling through the air wishing to grasp a trapeze,
then suddenly all depart with ease.

Metal violently collides with porcelain.
Paint freely splatters.
Mercy! What does it matter?

The impersonator wraps the tub's edge about.
The twisted ladder springs upright
with a snap and a shout!

Crumpled on her back, the painted lady lies,
stunned, scared, winded.

No doubt Michelangelo
would be disappointed she was fully clad.
What a mishap she just had!

Let's just say, if padded plywood weren't placed over the tub, the impersonator's back might have snapped in half.

Does the injured babe dare move? One leg dangles over the edge; tangled with a miserable dancing partner. Painted lady's back screams to reposition.

In the past, this gal simply prayed over her body, got up, and was done. This time, however, instructions had been given in advance. Conscious, moaning, and gasping for air, the dazed one grabs the two-way-communicator, slowly rolls off the tub, and follows orders.

"911, how can I help you?"

"I just fell off a ladder."

"Ma'am, do you always sound this shallow? Your breathing, I mean."

"No." Tears gently roll down stunned cheeks. I feel and hear the strain for every breath. The operator and I discuss how to enter the house without breaking down the door.

"You can hang up now. Help is there."

Impersonator burst into tears. "Thank you."

It's not that this incident is tragic or anything close. Several years ago the fire department responded to this very address. Bobbi called 911 when she was in serious trouble. She didn't make it.

No wonder a parade of neighbors shows up alongside the team of paramedics.

Handsome EMT's swirling about are too much for these eyes to bear. All Michelangelo can think is, *sure glad no one had to feast their eyes on a naked painted lady.*

Familiar voices call from down the hall.

"Reneé, is that you? Are you okay?"

"Glad I put on clothes before the party got started."

Nervous laughter echoes down the hallway over the silly comment.

Making the best of an awkward situation one of the firemen injects, "My friend Russ paints naked too."

"Ooo, stop! Don't make me laugh. It hurts too much." Ribs, back, muscles, every fiber of my being feels the impact of the fall mixed with awkward laughter.

Not sure how muscular hunks move a banged-up, fully clad painter from a cramped bathroom, but I find myself shivering on the adjacent bedroom floor with a brace strapped around my neck.

Pulse taken. Heart rate checked. And whatever EMT's do.

Now if I were single, this is a moment to savor. Could make a girl's head spin. As a happily married woman lying on the floor in distress, appreciation for lifesavers carries a much different flavor.

Our neighbor, Gale, who frequently refers to Richard as "Mr. Always Right" (case in point), takes it upon herself to phone Rich at work.

Won't he be surprised?

"Hey, Richard, Reneé fell off the ladder. They are taking her to the hospital." A slight pause, "Richard is on his way," Gale reports.

"Thanks, Gale." Without ever seeing her, I knew who took such good care of us.

"One, two, three!" Several hunks strain to lift the limp body. The crowd parts as the Red Sea for the fully clad Michelangelo and her good-lookin' escorts.

Wake me when the excitement is over.

I recall the crackle of my rescuers' two-way communicators as they ask, "Where do you want to go, Reneé?"

"Not Lutheran Hospital."

"Okay, we won't take you to Lutheran. How about if we take you to Littleton?" Littleton Hospital is only minutes away.

"NO! Don't take me there." The fall has obviously affected my brain cells as names of hospitals escape me.

"Umm, take me to Swedish."

"Why do you want Swedish?" No doubt, the EMT speculates I've lost my mind. "Swedish is a lot further."

Clarity shatters the blur. On many occasions, Richard and I had discussed in the event of an emergency NEVER use Littleton Hospital.

Overcome, I choke back tears and mumble to the EMT, "Littleton is where my husband's first wife and mother died. Don't take me there; it would kill him."

While his fallen bride is in transit, Richard prays in the powerful manner he recently learned. "There will be no broken bones and no repercussions of this fall. In Jesus' name."

According to the X-rays, it is a rather dull event.

Mr. Right retrieves his strong-willed, uninjured wife.

"There are no broken bones, nor fractures. In fact, we can't find anything wrong. She is free to go." The attending physician signs my release. "I'll write a prescription for pain pills. She will surely need them," the doc emphatically expresses.

The tough babe declares, "I'll be fine, Doc. I don't need any."

"I'll give it to you anyway, just in case," the persistent Doc assures Ms. Stubborn what to expect. Mr. Right takes the prescription, squeezes my hand, leans over the emergency bed, and whispers in my ear, "I anticipated nothing less."

We filled the script but never used it. The painted lady had no pain but was plenty sore.

I told the doc I didn't need it. It's how I roll.

Here I am amidst revising this chapter when whisked away to paint. Wish me well.

Speak to the Storm

It's show-n-tell, Jesus style! Wish this was in my tool belt years ago. Life might have looked different. Listen up!

Jesus and his disciples venture off to sea when a violent storm disrupts their cruise. Panicked disciples awaken Jesus, begging for something to be done before they lose their lives.

This colorful short story reaches far beyond the comfort of His followers. It's deeper. Pay attention!

Jesus arose and spoke directly to the turbulent wind and waves lapping over the boat. He commanded the storm to be still. And it was. That's right, He just spoke to the storm, and it obeyed.

Read the story for yourself in Matthew 8:23-27.

NEWS FLASH for the hungry! Revelation might slap you dumbstruck as it did me: Jesus didn't do signs and wonders just to impress or gather a crowd. NO.

He did signs, wonders, and miracles to show us how we also could walk in signs and wonders. Remember He told us "with God all things are possible" if you believe (Matthew 19:26 NIV). Pretty incredible, really. Unheard of for many. I know.

Why not learn from the greatest of teachers?

Jesus said, "whoever believes in me will do the works I have been doing, and they will do even greater things than these" (John 14:12 NIV).

One day when I was struggling with something significant, the Spirit of God said, *"Reneé, it is one thing to know the Word, another to believe the Word, and another to walk it out."*

What good is knowledge if not applied to life? Everyday opportunities come along to apply knowledge. Let's fix our broken believer. Stop listening to those who tell us contrary.

TRUTH NEVER CHANGES.

This story is not a fable. This experience happened several times regarding weather. Pay close attention, for the concept reaches beyond hectic storms.

Here it goes… buckle up!

A train trip from Silverton to Durango is in the making.

"Plush vintage car seats are sold out, Luv." Bummer, that was part of the experience.

"Babe, if you're interested, we can get tickets for an outside car."

Nothing sounds glamorous about a wooden bench, open air, soot producing historic train. At least the caboose is covered.

"Just do it. We'll be fine. It'll be fun." The flexibility of a discriminating engineer surprises me. He tells me how quick and ready to switch directions at any moment he is. I struggle to see it, but sure enough, he tickles me so.

September thunderheads threaten our trip. Our parched state is desperate for water. Not to be selfish but our safety is at risk. Corvettes don't handle well on wet roads and jeopardize dazzling hot-rod pizzazz.

"Lord, let the rain be anywhere but where we are, according to Mark 11:24, 'Whatever you ask in prayer, believe that you have received, and it will be yours.' Thank you."

We don't care if it rains, just not on us or the shiny Corvette. What can I say? Yes, we're spoiled.

Day one: Colorado's cobalt sky turned dreary grey.

Day two: sky remains dismal.

Again, we pray, "It can rain anywhere but where we are. In Jesus' name, amen." It's all about keeping the car clean and us dry. Pathetic, I know.

The minute we board the train, it pours. Rain obscures the mountain scenery. Not ideal, but captivating. Evergreens poke through dewy clouds. Smell the fragrance of a drenched forest. So refreshing to the soul.

Unexpected. Breathtaking. Postcard worthy.

One could say, "See, you got rained on!" But we didn't. Protected under the caboose overhang, we snuggle together fascinated by the picturesque scenery. Perfect!

Yikes! Don't look down. There is nothing, I repeat NOTHING holding this train up but tracks. Like floating in the clouds.

Timed to perfection, rain slows to a drizzle. The coal-fired train chugs to a stop in the historic town of Silverton.

What an unexpected photo opportunity! *Click, click, snap, snap.* Hazy days lend authenticity to create vintage-looking photographs. "Luv, stand next to the train for a shot. Perfect."

"Now, let's find a place to eat."

Snobs turn their noses up at several ordinary eateries before stumbling upon a peculiar window. Stop. Peer. AH. A quirky place worthy of our business.

Mr. Budde holds the door for his bride. What can I say, he's a dying breed. Creaky wooden floors welcome the snobs.

"Oh, my!" gawks the awestruck one.

Handlebar's Saloon is certainly a boisterous establishment. Enticed by luscious aromas, and an eclectic assortment of humanity. We can't help but notice the veil of webs swaying from ginormous tattered mounts to wee-little ones. Ambience in spades! A quirky place worthy of our business. We're suckers for old, odd and peculiar, I guess.

Check out the burley Harley dude sitting at the bar wearing his chick magnet. Who would've thunk a woolly old biker dude strutting a yak fur vest and a Viking helmet would be such a crowd pleaser. But he is. Watch the babes swarm.

Prior to selfies and cell phones, spectators were snagged to capture the moment. I'll give it my best shot. Enthralled is the hot chick. Certainly, the geezer gets pleasure in all the attention.

Sheets of rain pour down the windowpane as we indulge in people watching, giant juicy burgers, and bread pudding. Mercy me! To this day, the BEST-EVER bread pudding to touch my lips. Slathered in Jack Daniels whiskey sauce! None compares. None. Nowhere.

Looking out the rickety saloon door, Richard reminds the torrential downpour, "Be gone!" He turns and signals, "Let's go" and swings the door open. The rain abruptly stops.

Leaving Handlebar's Saloon, cigarette extinction bucket catches our eye. "The liver is evil; it must be punished!" We chuckle and snap a shot.

"Seems to be working," he says as we meander through freshly drenched streets, jumping over potholes filled with mountain rain. Do you smell it?

"ALL ABOARD!" cries the conductor.

To declare "Whatever you ask in prayer, believe that you have received, and it will be yours" (Mark 11:24) worked swell.

As the train pulls away, the clouds open with yet another deluge. Jesus sure knows how to put on a show. Life in abundance is an amazing state of being.

Storms don't always appear like rain, floods, or tornados. Storms might resemble family or workplace dynamics, health issues, or a turbulent distraction.

Wonder Boy

According to my cousin there isn't a man alive who hasn't done it.

I can't believe all men have done this. Not to mention, live to talk about it. Why would any man intentionally do this to himself? Don't men use their heads? Yes, that's a bit rhetorical.

Most men don't intentionally endanger themselves. Nothing short of a miracle. He should be dead.

Don't get me wrong, a fair share of women do stupid too. After his near-death experience, we heard of many men doing the very same thing. Some don't live to tell their story.

After my husband was laid off, he took a fond liking to micromanaging his self-sufficient wife. For the salvation of our marriage, Road Apples was created. For the benefit of those with no idea what road apples are, it's an old-fashioned term for horse poop.

Road Apples truck 'n' trailer

People stop all the time to discuss the creative logo on the side of his dump truck. Sorry, I can't divulge the masterpiece. Just know, it's a showstopper. Let's explore what happened.

Richard was hired to shuffle piles of manure for a ranch outside of town.

When the phone rang, I was up to my armpits in paint.

Darn, I missed my Hunny's call!

Hmm, the message undertone sounds a bit frazzled. "Come get me" is hardly adequate information. Did he blow a tire or an engine?

Ring! Ring!

"Richard, where are you?"

Muffled, barely audible between blitzes, I catch, "Come get me!"

"Where are you?"

Multiple attempts to convey his whereabouts before vaguely recognizing "SEDALIA!"

I yell back, "TEXT ME YOUR ADDRESS," as if hearing loss is the issue. What an opportunity for Mr. Budde to implement his newly acquired skill.

If an exclusive ranch is where I'm headed, appropriate attire is a must. Neither my man nor my leather seats appreciate being wallered in crusty paint, a trait I've picked up being married to the man of perfection and detail.

Old Iris turned into a sleek pearl-white turbo-charged hotrod. The LWC (little white car) as Richard fondly refers to it awaits the painted lady decked out in attire worthy of a swanky equine ranch.

Traffic is slow as molasses. Richard will have to wait. Some lessons never fade. No good can come of an empty gas tank. LWC rolls into the gas station. NO, I didn't stop for a latté! But I could have. The mystery ranch is an hour's drive.

Halfway to Sedalia, another text arrives. It reads: "the ambulance is on its way."

Ambulance! "For what!? For whom!? For you!?"

Silence follows.

Maybe his fingers are broken.

Cell reception is deplorable. Road lines fade into oblivion. My mind plays havoc with wild speculation.

Richard sounded okay.

I shoot off a text: "Should I meet you somewhere?"

"The barn."

There you go. An opportunity to rendezvous at the hospital was given, yet I'm directed to the barn. It can't be that bad.

According to Google maps, the ranch is close.

Flashing lights whiz past going the opposite direction. *Richard is in that ambulance.* I'm certain. Should I turn around and follow or go to the barn?

Do as you're told wins the argument.

Frustrated, spinning donuts on Google's tiny blue dot, "Where is the entrance!?" I'm ready to slap somebody.

FINALLY! Two ambulances emerge from the weeds, to illuminate the ranch's hidden entry.

"Hey, I'm looking for Richard Budde. Can you tell me where he is?"

"He just left in that ambulance."

"What happened?"

"He was crushed by his dump truck. He's been taken to Littleton Hospital. The police are waiting for you at the barn."

Jolted by the casual delivery of being crushed. "Okay, thank you."

Littleton Hospital would not be of his choosing. It's been discussed many times. NEVER go there. Even you know that!

Bumping over the washboard driveway simulates my gut. Nestled amidst the valley floor trees, a large red barn inundated by a barrage of emergency vehicles awaits the distressed wife. Not a welcoming committee for a hang nail.

The LWC skids to a halt next to the officers.

"Are you Reneé?"

"Y . . . E . . . S" chattered teeth sputter. Shock sets in over the sight of emergency vehicles.

"W-h-a-t h-a-p-p-e-n-e-d?"

"Oh, he suffered a *slight* injury," casually describing a much less impactful version from that given by the ambulance driver. "He got tangled between a gate and the dump truck."

Moving onto other matters of importance, "What's Richard's date of birth? And your address?"

"Where did they take him?"

"Littleton Hospital. He's in good hands. Do you know where the hospital is?"

"Yes, yes I do."

Matter-of-factly, the officer asks more questions before releasing me to chase down my injured husband, warning, "Now don't drive like a maniac. He's conscious and coherent. Again, Rich is in good hands."

Clouded by shock, I cling to the officer's lingering words. It's the longest half-hour drive of my life. Rattled by the reality staring us in the face. How life can quickly change.

How do stunned fingers make emergency calls?

Richard's daughter, Bridget, beat me to the ER and together we waited in an empty room. The authoritative voice in the hallway giving directives belongs to her father. Not sure if physicians appreciate patients questioning their every move. He can't help himself.

He's alert and sounds perfectly normal, other than repeating the phrase: "God saved me."

Physicians huddle to discuss Wonder Boy's injures while inquiring minds want to know, what happened? I'm with you.

Test results reveal several fractured vertebrae, multiple broken ribs, a broken right collar bone and crushed left forearm.

Bridget inquires, "Dad where was the safety manager?" referring to one of her father's numerous areas of expertise.

Rich didn't have a chance to respond before loud mouth blurts, "The safety engineer obviously didn't show up for work today! I cannot believe what you did to yourself!"

Mad but thankful he's alive, we pray, "Lord, thank you for saving Richard. May there be no repercussions of this injury."

"God saved me!" Wonder Boy declares with great enthusiasm. I've never seen my man this passionate.

Cowboy Up!

"COWBOY UP!" his bossy wife proclaims. "You'll be just fine. You've been caught being stupid."

Now before you slap me for being cold-hearted toward my husband's plight, just know there's more to the story.

This man I adore has no tolerance for incompetence or stupidity. If you choose not to impart grace for those who flow in stupid, the same is extended to you.

"It's simple, if you want mercy, give it. That's that," says the bossy one.

Inquiring minds must wait. Surgery takes precedence to knowing what happened that fateful day, the sixth of May. Repairs to the shattered arm go without incident.

Barely out of surgery, the curious one is ready to blow up. "What happened?"

"God saved me!" he explains. "It was the last load of the day." Rich takes a sip of water. "I was shuffling manure from one pasture to another. Opening and closing two sets of cattle gates. Both dump truck and trailer were fully loaded."

Keep in mind; cattle gates are heavy-duty, built to withstand huge pressure from livestock. Richard's equipment weighs twenty-six thousand pounds fully loaded. By day five, according to Wonder Boy, "the predominantly smooth and level terrain became familiar, other than tire ruts," which justified not using the emergency brake. "Saves time," don't you know?

Think of the gates as French doors, they latch together in the center. User is to lock the gates to prevent horses from escaping.

Richard explains how he developed a routine to avoid wasting time setting the brake or putting the truck in gear. "I'd stop, verify stability, jump out, unlatch and throw the gates open or closed, return to the cab, and drive straight ahead."

"On the last trip, both trailer and truck are chock-full. I pulled the truck and trailer past the first set of gates. After clearing, I slid out of the truck to secure the panels. The first gate surrendered to my push and stopped at the halfway point. I escorted the remaining gate to the center, then secured a chain to the companion gate."

Here's where it gets messy…

Unbeknownst to Richard, the truck and trailer were silently rolling backward and caught him mid-pivot, pinned sideways against the cattle gate.

Like tree branches, Richard's frame snapped.

How does one describe flirting with death?

"I knew my very existence was slipping away. To know I'm at the finish line, possibly my last breath, I gasp, God save me."

Like a Hollywood script, the latch broke. Gates hurl open, releasing his crushed body to the ground, escaping death.

"Thank God, I survived!" Gratitude floods Wonder Boy's soul. However, celebration was short-lived.

No Hollywood script could have conceived what happened next. Too preposterous for some to believe.

"Unable to move, I watched the truck slowly roll towards my motionless body. The truck tire aimed directly toward my skull! The rear bumper shadows overhead."

"I expected the worse." Inches from death, "waiting for the inevitable. Unexpectedly, the truck and trailer jackknifed. Saved twice!" the injured one declares.

"Stunned, lying on the ground, I knew I was seriously injured. I cried out, 'God, thank you for saving me.' Painfully I scooted to the gatepost, grabbed the rail, and pulled myself up."

"God heal me. No swelling, no bruising, no pain, no broken bones, and no repercussions,' I prayed."

Drawn to his feet, Wonder Boy inspected the hitch for damage before enduring the painful hoist back into the truck's cab. He bumped along the dirt road to the next pair of gates. A repeat performance: slide out, unlatch, throw the gates, jump back in, drive past the gates, jump out, gather gates, and latch.

Painfully, Richard climbed back into the truck multiple times, all while severely crushed. Work ethic and shock are the only explicable reasons he continued before strength gave way.

Limbs began to scream, "ARE YOU NUTS? STOP!"

Crushed survivor leaned against the trailer fender, dug out his phone and left the garbled message, "Come get me."

Ten minutes later, help arrived. Not me, but a ranch hand.

"Many people die of internal bleeding from the injuries Richard suffered," the EMTs said. According to the fireman overseeing the 911 response, "The EMTs were quite concerned."

Thankfully, I was not apprised of his critical condition.

The nurse interrupts story time and politely declares, "Mr. Budde, a rehab center is in your future. Monday is your release date. Remaining bones will heal on their own. Nothing further can be done."

Rehab falls on deaf ears. Resistance sets in.

Resilient man that he is, he cinched his Cowboy-up stance. If unfamiliar with that terminology, it's just another way of sayin' he sucked it up!

"I'm going home. What will it take to make that happen?" the resistant one asks.

Skeptically, the nurse rattles off a list for the injured, "Your oxygen needs to stabilize; you must be able to move about. The spinal block has to be removed, etcetera, etcetera, etcetera."

A spinal block was inserted to aide in his breathing due to all the broken ribs.

Adamantly, Wonder Boy informs his nurse, "That's what I'll do. There is no rehab center in my future!"

More light is shed on the miraculous event with each passing day.

Transformation is happening before my eyes. Richard has gone from hoping God hears, to believing God hears, to knowing God hears. All that mocking and ridiculing over wasting God's time with menial tasks, such as front parking spaces, has paid off. Remember?

Faith has taken hold, big time! It's how he rolls.

"Reneé, when I pulled myself off the ground, I spoke over my body. I knew I was hurt real bad but proclaimed, 'there will be no broken bones, no pain, no swelling and no repercussions from this injury.' God saved me!"

Blown away by the miracle lying in the hospital bed.

"You'll be fine," I say, agreeing with the cowboy up prayer.

Richard reinforces, "I'm going home, not to no stinkin' rehab center. I'll do whatever it takes to make that happen."

Every day the release date changes. Monday is scratched off. Sunday marked off. Saturday it is. No rehabilitation center for Wonder Boy! Instead, he heads straight home. Discharged three days earlier than planned, as declared, and believed.

Slap those nurses surprised.

What an extraordinary display of cowboy up!

That Mr. Budde sure is impressive!

Astounded

"Expect a therapist to drop by to start in-home rehabilitation, five days a week for a solid month," the voice informs the injured one over the phone.

Instructions to care for one bashed-up self with two broken wings, broken back, and multiple fractured ribs is underway.

Those occupational therapists sure know their business. Mr. Budde is self-sufficient in a matter of a couple of days. He's a quick study. I told you he was impressive.

Despite constant prayer over the clavicle, the agony is unbearable. The fractured bone protruded a good inch. In front of the bathroom mirror, the crushed one stands ready to battle. Fingertips glide over the discolored area—from muddy green, to eggplant, to soft yellow—across his chest and neck.

With grit, Richard gently lays hands on the bump, "God, we need to talk about this protruding bone and the constant pain. I've spoken over this bruise and pain, yet it remains. This should not be." Richard takes authority and declares, "Clavicle bone, I command you to line up with the Word! I speak to pain, swelling, and bruising. Be cast into the sea. Healing, health and restoration come into this body!"

Exhaustion follows the battle.

That evening, his beloved nursemaid remarks on the notable progress. "Luv, where did the discoloration go? And the huge bump? It looks nearly normal. What happened?"

"God and I had a chat. Within hours both the purple and the pain left. I wondered if you'd notice." Proudly he taunts, "and the clavicle no longer sticks out."

Slowly skimming my fingers over the much-improved area I marvel. "A-M-A-Z-I-N-G! Your bone has dropped down at least a half inch from this morning."

Another physical therapist arrives on the second day. Consistently glancing between the doctor's report and Richard, questioning, "are you really this injured? Most people who sustain these injuries don't look as good as you."

"It's God!" credits the glowing one.

Day three, yet another physical therapist arrives. I sit next to Richard at the dining table for a front row seat. Gently and slowly she sways his arm back and forth gradually extending the reach.

Annoyed, Richard inquires, "What are you doing?"

"Rotation. This prevents loss of mobility," the therapist responds. "Doctor's orders."

"Why are you wasting my time?"

"What do you mean?" quizzes the therapist, "show me what you are capable of."

Wonder Boy extends both arms into the air and flails them around as if ready to party. It's how he rolls.

Slapped astounded, the therapist packs up her bag of tricks from the greatly shortened session.

We can't help but laugh.

By evening of the third day, the therapist called, "Mr. Budde, you are released from rehab."

The surgeon's visit wasn't much different. "Wow! The physical therapists have done wonders."

"Oh no, I was released after three sessions."

How does one describe the body language of a doctor in shock and awe at the miracle he cannot deny? After the good doctor picked up his astonished jaw from the floor, he commented, "Richard, people your age (sixty-three) don't recover from this serious of an accident."

"I'm telling you; it's God! He saved me and healed me!"

A wild question follows, "Will I be able to spring to my feet from the floor like a ninja warrior?"

"Were you able to before?"

"Hell no! I just wondered if I could now."

No matter how impressive this man is, God is more. Give God a chance to show off.

People tend to rely on doctors. Believe it or not, Doctor Jesus can do what others can't.

Just sayin'. It's all in the book.

Music to My Ears

Six weeks from the impressive death defiant trick, Wonder Boy rides again! He's back to haulin' manure and in hot pursuit of a kitchen remodel project. Pretty amazing, huh?

We never hire contractors. We do it ourselves, with our own sweat! Well, mostly Wonder Boy's sweat. Don't underestimate his beautiful assistant's contribution.

All-inclusive remodelers, a.k.a. Team We, are killin' it! Our favorite part, writing those ginormous checks.

Richard installing the kitchen cabinets

Follow the storyline as we transition from kitchen to the theater's stage, closing scene. Anticipation rises. Zoom in on the stunning white cabinets standing erect against the wall, playing second fiddle to the enormous flamboyant black beauty island taking center stage. She's a looker alright! Glimpses of merlot peek beneath her distressed ebony finish.

A real diva she is.

Anticipation rises. It's the grand finale. A half dozen Russian hunks dance around Diva, before draping her with a gorgeous slab of Alaskan granite.

Smitten by Diva's beauty, we inquire, "Will she need legs?"

In broken English, the lead Russian throws his head back and chuckles. Then educates the unknowing about granite overhang dynamics. Vehemently he waves both hands beneath the island's empty space, "More ten inch need corbel. No leg, granite break."

Diva's top extends a whopping twelve inches.

Our plan to fit four barstools beneath is destroyed. By two inches! You've seen those bulky corbels. It's not the look we're after. Diva's grand finale is spoiled!

Attempting to reason with the Russian, "If skinny legs are used, maybe three stools can be squeezed beneath?"

The Russian boss knows we are not happy. He reiterates, "Scale all wrong. BIG island, granite heavy, need BIG leg."

We're not buying it.

Neither Richard nor I take kindly to being told what to do. This is no exception. Average is lame. Why settle for ordinary when extraordinary is obtainable? One of many qualities we love about each other.

Our house entry is a bit peculiar. Typically, you'll walk into a vestibule or grand entry. Not here. Guests are greeted by eye candy, the maître d', otherwise known as the Diva, or kitchen island. If legs are necessary, they need to be special, a statement, not an eyesore.

You should know by now that I discuss everything with God. That I share my displeasure over a lousy BIG leg mandate, should come as no surprise. It might seem silly to some to talk to God about such trivial matters.

Nothing is too trivial for Him. Nothing.

A few nights later, I have a dream. In this dream, Diva shows off slender clarinet legs. I know right? What a minimalistic solution! With instructions, too. Inserted through the center of the clarinet for strength was a steel rebar rod. Beautiful silver keypads harmoniously blend nickel hardware already installed on the wall cabinets. Music to my ears.

Talk about original! A piano, a saxophone, now clarinets. Fits the music theme sprinkled throughout the house. I'd bust a gut to come up with such an idea. God's originality shines!

Our finished kitchen remodel following Richard's horrific accident

Richard builds the showstopper legs. For a gimped-up fella, he does mighty fine work. And I helped.

Between the Giver of Dreams and Wonder Boy's ability, the kitchen turned out exceptional, if I do say so myself.

Nice, huh?

Give Diva and the chorus line a standing ovation. And Wonder Boy too.

Down 'n Dirty

Being an appreciator of all things dramatic, season tickets to Denver's prestigious Buell Theater is a pleasant perk. Seldom do we read what critics say. We don't care. Expectations lead to disappointment. We just go.

On the last Saturday of every production, you'll find us in the same glorious seats, where sweat and spit flies and scuffed dance shoes win the hearts of the audience.

Phantom's costumes took our breath away. *Wicked* was wickedly clever. Disney's *Lion King* lights up the stage with phenomenal talent, presentation, and unbelievable lifelike costumes. Don't bother with the knockoff version. *Jersey Boys* leaves one singing and dancing in your seats. *Jekyll and Hyde* will make your sides ache. *Little Mermaid* ignites awe and wonder.

Tonight's show is unfamiliar.

Before curtain call, a scantily clad actress artistically seduces a pole. Wide-eyed, I glance toward the ticket holders sitting next to us.

"Yeah, this one's a little raunchy," the gals comment with a squint and a shrug. "*Cabaret*."

Surprised by the suggestive pole dance, "Well, I guess."

The orchestra begins. Lights dim.

The escapades have barely begun. Behind backlit sheets, several participate in what should be private. It is all I can do to endure the first act. Now, I am not a prude, but I don't want to be subjected to lewdness of any kind.

Just yesterday the media lambasted Donald Trump for his vulgar locker room talk caught on tape. His comments weren't nearly as vulgar as what the audience just witnessed in Act One. By intermission, I'm disgusted!

The ladies sitting next to us inquire, "Are you going to stay?"

Mr. Budde responds, "Of course."

His response ignited a tongue on fire. Oh, the poor souls held captive in the twenty-eight-hundred seat auditorium designed for incredible sound travel. The voice of outrage interrupts intermission chatter, "THE HYPOCRICY OF OUR NATION NAUSATES ME! We crucify a man for filthy locker-room talk, yet clap for ninety-minutes of filthy production. If Donald had an orchestra and dancing girls behind him, would we have applauded?"

The answer to that rhetorical question is YES! YES! YES, we would have.

Now, I am not a fan of the man, but what Donald said in a private conversation is none of our business. Yes, it was NASTY. But the hypocrisy is blatant. A pivotal moment in the life of a theatergoer. Hopefully, everyone heard me LOUD and CLEAR that night.

Mr. Budde calmly replies, "I guess we are not staying. Goodnight, ladies." He gathers his livid wife and beelines it to the door.

While waiting for the train, I notice many theater programs in a chokehold.

Shy of midnight, the one on fire storms through the front door straight to the phone. "HOW DARE YOU SUBJECT US TO YOUR VULGAR PLAY WITHOUT ANY FOREWARNING." I threaten, "AFTER THIRTY YEARS, WE WILL NOT BE RENEWING OUR SUBSCRIPTION."

We did stay one more season, to catch the highly touted Hamilton. Afterward, we were finished. Done.

Possibly others expressed their infuriation. Because after Cabaret, we received notification of objectionable content. Sometimes, it just takes standing up for what's right. If we remember what that is.

Confidence

A bunch of writers and wannabes are sitting around the table, some are strangers, others just strange. Writers are challenged by the speaker with an interesting exercise: "Gather into small groups and tell each other specifically what you notice about one another."

A lady looks directly at me and says, "You are confident."

Astonished, "Now, how do you pick that up?" I asked.

"Because I don't have it."

Rather presumptuous of me, but unashamedly I ask, "Why not?" After all, shouldn't confidence be a natural byproduct of time? Time is on this gal's side.

Frankly, the lady discloses, "As a child, my mom questioned every decision I made. Which to this day, causes me to question my choices. You seem so decisive."

The conversation strikes me as odd.

A child's confidence destroyed by the actions of a well-meaning mom, stunned I am. This woman continues to bear the scars as an adult. To second guess every decision handicaps one for a lifetime.

Days later, while shopping in the craft store, the confident one stumbles upon a little guy's mama asking him to pick out a color for a project. Gray was his choice.

"Are you sure?" mom innocently questions the tike. "Maybe you'd rather have a more colorful one, like this one or that one." The mom undermines the child's selection.

I could bear it no longer and left the aisle.

Does she not see how undermining her child's decisions will destroy his confidence? Evidently not.

Had I not witnessed the long-term effects days earlier, I would not have recognized it either.

You know what that mama needs? Yep.

Sometimes hearing God's voice is not in your face but more subtle.

Answers

Having nearly given up, I prayed relentlessly for a chronically sick child to be made whole. Nothing doctors did or prescribed worked. They always came up empty.

My prayers had to change. But how?

Desperate, I ask, "Lord, how should I pray?"

In the middle of the night, the glorious answer manifested. I flung out of bed to jot it down.

May the answer given below deliver huge benefit to those seeking answers for themselves or your loved one.

Precious one,

This morning I asked how to specifically pray for you, and this is the result. This exercise is meant for you to implement.

You have tried EVERTHING under the sun, so why not give this a go?

Think of life as layers of an onion, with all its pungent aromas and tears. In this exercise, the object is to label, address and peel off each layer separately. Feel free to start from any direction, just as they come up in your thoughts. There is no right or wrong order or answer.

Listed below are a few examples I saw while praying. Address as many or as few topics at a time as you like. You'll know the right amount. Like anything worth doing, this will take effort. Allow time for other issues to come forth. As they do, address them in a similar manner.

Words spoken over me by _____ have no power over my body. I release the words _____ and their effects from attachment to any place in this body, mind, or soul. (Repeat this for different people and different words.)

Holy Spirit, come fill those wounds, holes, crevices with peace, joy, contentment, and your love. This invitation is just as important as the action it follows.

Food trauma. I speak to you, "You no longer have power over my body. I render you powerless. I am free of trauma over food. Body, mind, and soul, you will process food in a healthy manner. You are free from guilt or shame. Body, release the extra pounds my body doesn't need."

Holy Spirit, satisfy my hunger inside. Fill me to overflowing. Help me to see food as it was created.

Deeds done to me. I release and forgive _____ from doing _____ to me. Body, you will no longer hold on to that deed and the pain or trauma it caused. I release the effects (pain, trauma, broken heart) from my body. Pain, you leave my body. I kick you out, NOW! You no longer can take up residency here.

Holy Spirit, I invite you to fill the holes created by _____ with an overwhelming compassion for others who have suffered in this area.

I will not allow this event or person to control my thoughts any longer as I am FREE!

Memories that haunt me. No longer will you be given access or power to torment me. I speak to you and tell you to flee. Memories of _____ you are trespassing. I kick you out. You will not control this mind, body or will any longer. I will not be held your captive.

Holy Spirit, replace those memories with your perspective. Help me to see them entirely different. Replace and fill those places with pleasant memories.

Side effects of medications, treatments, etcetera, I speak to my body to line up with the Creator's design, to perform and function the way it was intended to. All side effects of anything taken into this body, seen and unseen, that have played havoc be null and void from this moment on. This body is perfectly and wonderfully made. Now, every internal function, every organ, every blood cell, function in harmony and perfection as you were intended. Invaders, you are not welcome in my body any longer. You are FIRED! You must exit now!

Now, Holy Spirit, You alone see what's happened internally. Restore me to wholeness.

Confusion, you will not take up residency in this body. I have clarity of mind. I am whole. I am loved by many, both now and in the future. I will walk in the design created for me. It is BIG. It is *wonderful*. It is *amazing*. I will not be confused and go astray from the gifts and plans placed inside. Any attempt to get me off the right path, be gone.

Holy Spirit, I ask You to implant into me Your plan and vision for my life.

I choose not to allow fear to control me any longer. Fear has no right to take up space in my head. God has not given me a spirit of fear but of power, love and a sound mind (2 Timothy 1:7). Fear of the known and unknown alike, fear, you are evicted effective immediately. Be gone! Every fiber in my being, I speak to fear and command my body to be released from all its side effects.

Spirit of the living God, fill me with peace to replace fear. The peace only You can give.

Holy Spirit, show me any other layers that need to be peeled away.

As He does, speak to them, tell them to leave your body along with their side effects. Then ask for the Holy Spirit to come and fill that vacancy with His love, peace, joy or whatever He deems fit to fill that space with.

Should any of these distant memories, pain, traumas, fears attempt to return, remind them they are trespassing and no longer allowed admittance into your soul, mind, or body. This may or may not happen. But if it does, after a couple of failed attempts, they'll stop tormenting you. John 10:10 tells us the "thief comes to steal and kill and destroy." If anything has that effect in our life, it is *not* of God but the enemy of our soul. The battle begins in our mind. We are transformed by the renewing of our minds.

Possibilities for consideration:

Anger

Depression

Nightmares

Betrayal

Abuse

Abandonment

Rejection

Self-hate

Declare it to be MY YEAR TO BE FREE!

LIFE BEYOND

The Present Realm

"In My Father's house are many rooms; if that were not so, I would have told you, because I am going there to prepare a place for you. And if I go and prepare a place for you, I am coming again and will take you to Myself, so that where I am, there you also will be. And you know the way where I am going." (John 14:2–4 NASB)

Walk Out of That Grave!

The unexpected call was devastating. "Charlotte is in the hospital. Cancer surgery was performed. Staph infection has set in. She's not doing well."

"Where is she? I must go to her."

A trach down her throat made holding a conversation virtually impossible. It was difficult to rise above what I saw much less believe for healing. But I had to. We all had to. Marvin, her anchor for nearly a century, stayed by her side hour after hour.

While she slept, I read the Bible to feed Charlotte's spirit. Anointing oil lay on a tray nearby. A host of friends wrapped Charlotte in prayer and anointed her on every visit. What an honor to walk through the valley of death with my dear friend.

On this visit, Char's doctor came into her room, so I stepped outside and overheard the conversation as I peered through the adjacent window. "Charlotte, you have completed your course. It's time for someone else to take over. It's time to give up."

Defiance arose from that sickbed. She wouldn't hear it. To give up would truly be the death of her. I prayed.

During Charlotte's yearlong hospital stay, she was said to have passed from this life FIVE times.

After defying the doctor's prognosis—cancer, staph and death—seventy-five years young, one-hundred-pounds lighter Charlotte, returned to South Africa. Her ministry flourished for yet another year before passing into glory. Big Mama left her indelible mark on so many lives.

Charlotte's impartation of selfless love and moving with the Spirit were foundational in my life. Taught by the best!

My priceless friend
Charlotte Cronk
A legend of love

"No one has greater love than this:
that he lays down his life for his friends."
- John 15:13 TLV

Edge of Eternity

Housed within the frail, hunched over aging body, resides a feisty, retired fourth-grade schoolteacher. Veroqua fears no one, not even strapping, athletic high school boys. It's nothing for her to call out misbehaving deeds with the strict teacher voice and the look.

Twenty-five years into retirement the five-foot white-haired shrinking teacher still owned it. You too would have jump if she asked. Don't be fooled by her gracious demeanor. She meant business.

Mrs. Smith's phone sizzled between neighbors, church, and Silver Sneakers. Her calendar was always packed.

Generations of students remained a vital part of her life. No wonder they adored her. Homemade wedding mints for students was her specialty.

She exuded kindness. Her favorite pastime was shuttling friends to appointments followed by lunch and laughter.

For the past several weeks, she's not been feeling her chipper self. Today's diagnosis seems incomprehensible. To discover your timeline is dramatically accelerated is not the way to begin a New Year.

Terminal heart disease creates a hiccup in one's plans.

Neither a heart transplant nor a valve replacement are feasible options. Palliative care is recommended.

Honor the brave woman for her choice. At the ripe old age of eighty-seven, no intervention will be pursued. On the edge of eternity, Mom pushes through to live another day, then another, then another.

She's not ready to disclose her condition to friends. Bad news always has been considered private, secretive, off-limits.

"Mom, you have poured into your friends for so long. Let them pour into you. People will want to know. They'll want to help, that is, if you'll let them."

Silence invades the room.

Word travels.

Many become unpleasant to be around as the curtain closes. Mother is truly an exception. Love, encouragement, affection, and palliative care merge on the corner of Davies and Sherman Streets.

Neighbors, friends, and former students frequent the ailing woman. Showering her cards, flowers and her favorite, fried okra.

I've never met anyone who doesn't respect and admire this feisty woman I call mom. Her impact shines brightly.

Richard frequently reminds me, "Your mom is really funny."

Annoyed, I snap, "No, no, no she's not. She just says and does stupid."

Mom drives me crazy. The schoolteacher continues to boss me around. I've owned a business for over seventeen years; by now she should've recognized something she taught me stuck. Her unsolicited advice is insulting.

With my propensity for violence, I'm slightly concerned about embarking upon my new role as caregiver. It would be tragic to lose patience and slap my own mother.

I need to get a grip.

"Lordy, Lordy! Help! Help me to treat Mom the way I'd want to be treated by my daughter."

Peace floods my soul, overtaken by a fresh perspective. Appreciation replaces annoyance. I never saw it before, but Mom is funny. My attitude adjustment is quick and painless.

Unbelievable, I know. It is all God.

When the palliative nurse asks, "Veroqua, are ready to enter hospice?" Mom replies, "I can't. I have too much food in the refrigerator."

Two weeks later the question resurfaces. "What would I do with all my stuff?"

"I told you," Richard nudges. "She's a hoot-meister."

When hospice introduces the idea of oxygen, Mom's caretaker fights it tooth and nail. "It's a dangerous trip hazard for an old lady living by herself," I justify.

"She'll be more comfortable," they insist.

Mom stands her ground! "Are you kidding? I don't want to be addicted to oxygen."

"Mom, I'm addicted to oxygen," my twisted brother claims.

Serious as a heart attack, Mom responds, "You are?"

What can I say? Mother makes us chuckle.

I was wrong, wrong, wrong! Oxygen is amazing! Oxygen gets five stars in my book! Mom's spunk and clarity returns.

Six months pass. The socialite's revolving door spins. Mom is failing hospice.

Hospice declares, "Chances are remote for your mom to remain at home. You should look for alternatives."

Well, by now you should know, I'm not buying that premise. My stubborn streak was inherited from my dad, or so I thought, until Mom's fortitude was displayed. No wonder I can't help myself!

Every effort to accommodate Mom's wishes to remain in her home is made.

I send up a short prayer, "Lord, don't let her die alone. I want to be there for her." Unbeknownst to me, her granddaughter Sunshine requests the same.

Mom doesn't want her untimely death to inconvenience my sister Denise's teaching schedule. It's a teacher connection, what can I say? Even in dying, Mom is considerate and practical.

Not to be selfish, but what about the self-employed caregiver ready to leave town for her husband's family reunion? What about that daughter's grueling schedule?

As director of all things pertaining to health and life, it's reestablished who gives orders. "Mom, there is absolutely no dying on birthdays. Just sayin' as mine is around the corner."

On the evening of my birthday, congratulations are in order, "Thanks Mom for not dying on my birthday."

"The day's not over yet." Mom sparred. Her spontaneous response still evokes a chuckle.

Her busy itinerary is of the upmost importance and is frequently discussed. "Family is coming for Sunshine's birthday dinner in three weeks. Later, there's the neighborhood picnic. There is no good time to die, Mom. Your social calendar is packed," says the no-nonsense schoolteacher's trainee.

Colorado has NEVER peaked at 105-degrees for days on end, until this summer! Without air-conditioning, Mom cannot endure these intolerable temperatures. It's time to correct the issue. So I do.

Begrudgingly, Mom tattles, "*Reneé* is spending my last dime."

"It's either air-conditioning or assisted living, Mother."

We both know a move isn't going to happen.

Action is taken. The terracotta brick house on Sherman Street buzzes with worker bees. The power was shut off all day yesterday to update the knob and tube electrical panel.

Handsome, hungry young bucks armed with toolbelts and a sense of humor take the edge off the smoldering days. Scavengers assist in the disposal of delectable homemade dishes found in the vintage frig.

Tranquility of daybreak is interrupted by the obnoxious noise of heavy hydraulics. Mom blows out of bed, trades the oxygen hose for a shiny red walker and rushes out the front door.

Headlines read: GRANNY CHASES TRASH COLLECTOR!

Ninety-pound grandmother asserts her authoritative teacher voice, "YOO-HOO! Come back! COME BACK!!"

Oops, busy daughters neglected to set out yesterday's stinky trash. Heroic neighbors rush to aid the fragile woman's quest.

It is a proud moment in the life of a hospice chick. Granny is last seen sporting a cotton nighty leading a sunrise parade down Sherman Street.

I'm telling ya, she's a hoot-meister, just as Mr. Budde said. He's always right you know. Just ask our neighbor Gale.

The Other Side

Mom is thriving six months into her hospice journey. My sister Gwen asks, "Do you think she doesn't want to see Daddy?"

Our obstinate father wasn't the easiest man to be around. He did his best to push people away. Some hated him, others tolerated him, most ignored him. Only an angel would remain married to the grumpy geezer for fifty-six years.

Daddy held claim to genius. Passionately he justified, "No one understood Einstein either." Unapologetically adding, "and I don't care what people think."

A gruff sort he was. His range of topics was religion and politics. And never open to receive another's viewpoint. It was always a one-way discussion. Always.

When we cleaned out daddy's belongings, we stumbled upon papers hidden in the dark. Slap me silly! He *was* a genius! As kids, we thought he was plain crazy. What do kids know?

Genius is no excuse not to show love and affection. A byproduct of that generation, I guess. Nevertheless, it caused irreparable damage to some.

Here's an opportunity to walk out some tough forgiveness.

Following Gwen's audacious idea about Mom not wanting to see Daddy on the other side, I had a vision. In the vision, Daddy was giddy with excitement at heaven's gate in anticipation of Mom's arrival. He didn't look or behave like the man I grew up with, but I knew it was him. He was much younger, and full of pure joy, attributes rarely if ever displayed on earth. The vision ended.

My perspective shifted of my grumpy father.

Originally, I perceived the vision was for the inquisitive sister. But as time progressed, clearly it was bigger. Much bigger. The vision brought me comfort as well. I hope it does the same for you, my friend.

Then I had another vision regarding my deceased son-in-law. He was a pathetic father and husband to my daughter and a poor role model to his children. You know the type.

In the vision, he too was in heaven. He was deeply remorseful for the way he treated his family. Thomas kept repeating the phrase, "Tell my family, I'm sorry for what I did to them. I had no idea of the impact of my actions."

This vision made me weep profusely as I realized the magnitude of the grudge I held against Thomas over the deep emotional scars left on his family.

No slap can erase a festered grudge. Particularly if they are deceased.

At that point, it became my issue in need of attention, not his. It broke me. Through tears I let his destructive deeds go.

Timing is Everything

Late Saturday afternoon phone calls start streaming into the salon.

"Reneé, I need to cancel Monday's appointment. Something has come up." Within twenty minutes, all appointments cancelled. This is highly unusual.

I sense change in the air.

On the heels of today's cancelations, Mom's friend and neighbor, calls, "May I sit with your mom Monday afternoon?"

"Hmm, I'm not sure, Mary Elizabeth." Realizing my hesitance could be misunderstood, a meager attempt to explain is given. "All of Monday's hair appointments canceled. I'll be at Mom's. On second thought, why not. Monday afternoon will be fine."

"Do you think something will happen to her?"

"I don't know. I only know my day has cleared."

"Two o'clock then?"

"Two o'clock will be fine. See you then." Click.

It's Monday, July 23 at 8:45 a.m. Today just feels different. Comfort and peace flood my body and soul under the hot shower. Before leaving the house, I give Richard a long tight embrace and kisses linger.

Calmly I proclaim, "Don't know when I'll be home. Today is Mom's day."

Mother has been doing extraordinarily well. There is no reason for me to conclude today will be any different. She's continued to thrive, entertaining visitors and chattering on the phone for hours.

Even though we live only five minutes apart, I call on the way over to verify all is well.

"Hello," whispers the faint voice on the other end.

Taken by surprise by the weakness in Mom's voice. "Mother, where is Elma? Is she there?"

The faint voice calls, "Elma."

"Mother, Mother?"

No dial tone. No Elma. No Mom. No panic. I walk in the front door and find mother resting in her new leather lounge chair, the phone cradled in her lap.

The house is peaceful and eerily quiet. There is no acknowledgment of my arrival.

"Elma?" How can Elma be lost? The front door opens and in she walks.

"I was looking for you."

"I just ran home to change clothes."

"Elma, let's move Mother to her bed." Slowly Mom walks between arms of assistance. We tuck her tired body into bed before sitting down for an update.

"Your mom did not sleep well last night. She kept flinging her leg over the side of the bed. I crawled into bed with Veroqua and held her through the night."

My heart melts. Can you think of a lovelier act of kindness or compassion? Elma has been a great neighbor and friend, and now Mom's comforter. Elma's affection toward my failing mother moves me so.

"Thank you, Elma, for all you do for Mom. Go home and get some rest. I'll stay."

"Are you sure?"

"We'll be fine. Get some rest."

Ten o'clock, no change, no response. I expect hospice sometime today. Nurse Mary should be apprised of Mom's condition.

Ring!

"Mary, what time will you arrive?"

"I'm in the midst of an emergency; I'll be there after eleven."

"Okay, thanks." No hurry. What could she do anyway?

Alone in the bedroom, I watch my sweet mama barely breathe. All activity has ceased. No calls. Nobody at the door. It's exceptionally quiet. As if the entire entourage knew this was her day.

Years ago, I prayed for Mama to live life to the fullest, up to her last breath. Never has the awareness of eternity been so tangible. Peace fills the quiet bedroom.

Nurse Mary arrives and is stunned by Mom's rapid decline. "The end could be several days away," the nurse informs me.

"No, Mary, today's her day."

Mary continues, "I'll call in a prescription. It'll be here in a couple of hours."

Did she not hear me?

"She won't need it."

Pay no attention to the daughter who knows nothing. Calmly I retort, "Do what you want." After all, Mary's the professional. I drop it.

"Call me, if you need anything," Mary walks out.

"Yes, thank you."

My brother and sisters have been calling daily to talk to mom. Now it's my turn to make the calls.

"This is it. If you want to talk to Mom, I'll hold the phone to her ear. She can hear you, but don't expect a response."

Sunshine and Grammy are extremely close. She's working today, yet I know it's important to call her.

"Mom, I'm on my way."

Calls are completed. Everyone got to say good-bye. There was no reaction from Mother as the whispers of love from her children flood her ear. Still and peaceful, Mother lays quietly propped up in the hospital bed. Somberness fills the room that only days before permeated with laughter.

The entire family visited the past weeks, reminiscing ghastly, unbelievable childhood memories. All four kids were raised in this home. It's the only place known to her grandchildren and great-grandchildren.

The weight of the end is sensed.

Richard walks in! Color me surprised!

"What are you doing here?"

"I thought about what you said this morning, about this being Mom's day. I knew I needed to come."

Comfort floods my soul to know Mr. Budde trusts my instincts. Richard leans over the bed to softly whisper, sharing his affection.

Ensuing Richard's arrival, Sunshine bounces through the bedroom door with a burst, "Grammy, I'm here!"

Mom's eyes spring wide open!

Softly Grammy mouths the words, "I love you," then closes her eyes to resume her tranquil state of being. WOW! I'm so moved.

Together we sit on the bed holding Mom's hand singing old hymns picked for her service. We muddle through "I Come to the Garden Alone." "Amazing Grace" is better. If a daughter had any sense, she would speak to her mother instead of tormenting the dying soul with poor lyric recall of unrehearsed hymns.

Mom probably thought, *STOP! You're killing me.*

She's spared by the doorbell. All exit the bedroom to greet Mary Elizabeth. While the four of us chat in the living room, Sunshine returns to check on Grammy, only to make an about face. "Mom! I think Grammy took her last breath!"

All sorts of legs race down the narrow hallway. Before we reach the entry, we hear the loudest exhale, as if wind departed from her body.

Silence followed. What a privilege to walk Mom to the edge of eternity.

Go!!

"*Go to him,*" the Spirit of God whispers. *"He's not long for this world."* Numerous times I've tried but was intercepted. It is now or never. In the hospital bed lies my ex-husband, suffering repercussions of a horrific massive stroke.

Ben took extreme measures to stay alive, except obedience to lay down the cigarettes. Remember the vision from the Chuck's Donuts days? He was told to quit smoking before God could use him for world evangelism.

Ben refused to stop smoking for anyone: me, his many fiancés, himself, or God. Choices have implications.

We all have demons to war against; they just look different. Ben's was smoking. Now don't presume God or I are against smokers. Neither will I pounce on you. This was Ben's fight. Obedience verses desire.

Finally, Ben did comply. But not before his health deteriorated beyond repair. A year ago, he had a mechanical heart implanted, a risky procedure to prolong his life.

The implanted heart device is the only reason he lives, although being confined to a hospital bed unable to walk or talk is not my idea of living.

You can imagine the shock when I walk into Ben's hospital room. Yours truly is not real comfortable either. This visit is a mission trip of sorts, not about my comfort.

Days earlier, the Lord spoke to me about the need to share *forgiveness* with the man of failed health. This mission is not about my forgiveness toward Ben, as I released that toxic tonic years ago, rather this is about unfinished family business.

Well, to carry on a conversation with a man who can't speak is much like old times, yet distinctively different. This time tremendous empathy accompanies me. I feel bad for the bedridden man who fathered our beautiful daughter.

"Ben, I'm here to talk about forgiveness."

In walks his male nurse—Awkward! I attempt to resume the conversation while vitals are taken, but this is way too personal.

Stop. Just stop.

The nurse offers, "If you wish, I can find the nurse in charge to share his health status."

"No. No, thank you, I'm here for other reasons." I turn my head and hold back tears. The nurse seems to linger in hopes to catch the one-sided conversation. Strained minutes pass. Two minutes turn into five; five stretches into a lifetime before the nurse completes his routine.

Breathe deeply, Reneé. "As I was saying, forgiveness is my purpose for being here today. You always thought I owed you an apology. Don't think for a minute you were without fault in our marriage. The reality is, I forgave you for what you did to me over those twenty-seven years.

"Ben, not everyone has forgiven you. You have three grown children who are very angry with you. You felt disillusioned by God, and I'm here to ask if matters are cleared up between you and God before you depart?"

Ben nods, but I'm not certain he understands. I know he hears even if he can't speak. The lights are on, but is anybody home? It's hard to tell.

"I'm sorry you're going out this way. May I pray for you?"

He shakes his head, seemingly no. What I came for is far more important than to cave over an indiscernible nod. *He might have meant yes. What's he going to do? Slap me?*

He can't speak; he has no choice. This woman on a mission will not be derailed. Standing alongside his bedridden body, I pray, "Lord Jesus, may mercy flow to Ben and beyond to his children for the hurt and anger caused. May it all melt away. May Ben forgive You for disappointments of a life that didn't go according to plan. Bathe this entire situation in Your loving forgiveness. In Jesus' name, amen."

I bend over Ben's clammy cold forehead and seal the prayer with a kiss and a quiet, "I love you."

I'm as shocked as you. It's inconceivable how or why those words left these lips, but they did. My work here is complete. Before walking out the door, I turn to say, "Tell Mom hello."

In the hallway I bawl.

Ben passed away several days later.

Note to self: We feel justified in holding onto betrayal. Truly, the one *not* willing to release, pays the greatest price.

FAVOR

Comes not because of how
wonderful you are but
because how wonderful HE is.

"A good man obtains favor from the LORD."
(Proverbs 12:2 ESV)

The Hunt

Every weekend Mr. Budde loads the yellow hotrod and off into the wild he whisks me away in search of an investment project with the Look. Not just any project. One with history. We've seen nasty. We've seen moldy. Mostly, we've seen those in need of a torch.

The goal is to be within an hour's drive. Both budget and drive time were set, reset, and set again. The only unchanging requirement was the Look.

The Look was paramount.

Does Mr. Budde really need another project? Repeatedly I apprise him, "There are plenty of projects to do right here, Luv."

That was a waste of oxygen. Jump on board, girl. Enjoy the ride. Your man is driven to find himself a gem.

Weekend warriors trot off to lands unknown. Traveling to the borders of Wyoming, Utah, and New Mexico in search of the Look.

The Internet creates desire. Desire needs fed. Desire costs money. Desire is greedy. How much money do you have? It's never enough.

In days of old, one sought professionals. Today, one surfs any time, any state, any location. For that matter, the entire globe is at our fingertips.

"It's all part of the hunt," I'm told. To explore territories unseen by the likes of us is fun. "Who doesn't enjoy being wined and dined all weekend?" Resembles a honeymoon. Winky, winky. And on a monthly basis. Sweet!

Inquiring minds want to know. What are you looking for?

This girl's only request is to be near water.

The Great Hunter's request is simple, "an outhouse would be just fine; a hand pump would be extravagant. Smaller is ideal, maybe two hundred square feet. Nothing cutesy."

He wants history. Miner, trapper, something to give it provenance. Old, log, and rustic. You know? The Look.

The sweetest little yellow summer cottage was spotted on the river in Boulder County. I LOVED IT! So what if the cottage has issues? We all have issues. Yes, it slopes toward the river. It isn't in the river.

This cottage needs both a new well and septic, and if it gets washed away, well, too bad. New ordinances won't allow for a rebuild, like the town of Lyons. But oh, it is CUTE! CUTE! CUTE!

Location, location, location! It didn't have the Look Mr. Budde sought. But Mrs. Budde's heart fluttered.

Countless were the cabins we saw over the next two years.

One fall weekend we head south to see a cabin with an old caboose. And another cabin, a real budget buster we'd seen online. It's way more cabin, way more money, and way past the allotted drive time. But has the Look.

Clouds sock the valley in, teasing us, hiding its beauty. Our overnight accommodations are charming. Not to everyone's liking, but we hold a fond appreciation for rustical. Tall pines whispering in the breeze, clanging screened porch doors, vintage furnishings all evoke nostalgia of another era.

Doing what we do, we proceed to explore the wide spot in the road. This enclave has a gas station, an itty-bitty liquor store, a post office, three small churches, and a restaurant. No stop lights or signs.

People wave as we pass by. We drive past a lady tending her flowers. Ferociously she waves.

Mr. Budde inquisitively turns and asks, "Do you know her? She acts like we should know her."

"Of course not, I've never been here before."

Not to be rude, we stop and visit, enjoy a glass of wine and her fabulous views off the deck. We tour her home, handle her guns, discuss boyfriends, local water boards, and the value of real estate in the valley before our sunset departure.

The following morning, we head over to the budget buster. As soon as we drive up the tree-lined drive, I turn to Mr. Budde and say, "You might as well write the offer now." This was EVERYTHING he'd been looking for and so much more. More square footage, more land, more money, more drive time. But it certainly has the Look in spades!

Walking through the front door, we are transported back in time. The massive beams, the charm, the character, the creaky floors all take our breath away. A massive stone fireplace with rope mortar built to impress does. A look not seen in any cabin until now.

Our 150-year-old homesteader cabin

The builder's superb carpentry skills are on full display. Hand-hewn logs perfectly dovetail together!

"Check out the sweet red vintage built-in buffet. Have you ever seen such charm? Brass hardware sets the tone, doesn't it?" as I dote.

"The modern light fixtures are all wrong, but that can be fixed," Mr. Budde comments.

"Mercy, who would apply gloss over the fireplace's pink stones? Seems so silly," the decorator observes.

Later we discover Beulah is the only place in the world those glazed pink stones, otherwise known as rose quartz are quarried. It's the same rose quartz on Colorado's state capital walls. Maybe that shine is natural? Or meant to draw attention. It does.

The remodeled kitchen hardly complements the hundred-fifty-year-old cabin. Too bad someone had no idea how to choose colors or, for that matter, paint. Paint is slopped everywhere. We can fix that too. Isn't this what Mr. Budde was looking for? A project?

NOW THAT'S WHAT I'M TALKING ABOUT! Tucked out back is exactly what we had in mind. But if we want that sweet little itty-bitty cabin in the back yard, the big cabin comes with it. A package deal. Like re-marriage with kids. Can't have one without the other.

This old, hand-hewed log cabin smells of history and a few less desirable scents, like dogs, bat guano, mice, skunks, clogged pipes, sewer. Unpleasant odors that keep potential buyers away, those kinds of odors.

"Did you notice the creek across the road? It's down slope. Can you believe it? And an incredible wrap around front porch. By the creek!"

"It's a *really* stinkin' big project, Mr. Budde."

We hunted for a rowboat and bought ourselves a cruise ship. We can't help ourselves. It's how we roll. We should be committed.

We couldn't be happier.

"Where're all the projects Richard's looking for?" you ask. Oh, there are plenty to address. The gutters have fallen off. The wasp infested skylight suffers a serious leak. Forty-year-old wallpaper clings no more. Fifteen shades of pink nail polish covers the bedroom's floor and walls. The list goes on and on.

Dark terra cotta and dingy gray are hardly my color choices for a kitchen or any place for that matter. It must go!

Now you might be tempted to run your hands over these very cool, rustic hand-hewn logs, don't! Nails and tacks cover every square inch. Makes for a bloody mess.

What a BIG project. Will we live long enough?

Divine Shopping

Other than a blow-up mattress, the cabin is empty. We barely left to go shopping when my phone rang with an unrecognized number. Rarely do I answer unidentified calls. But I did.

The soft voice on the other end declares, "The Lord told me to call and pray for you. What do you need?" asks my new friend.

WOW! Slap me surprised! The smallest of details don't get by the Great Provider.

"Yes! Please! We would love it! Richard and I are headed out for a nearly impossible task: To acquire an entire household of furniture for under five thousand dollars. Each piece needs to embody the Look, as if it lived all its life in a hundred-fifty-year-old cabin. We realize this is mission impossible. You're a doll, thank you for your prayers."

Impeccable timing!

The saving grace is not all rooms need to be furnished. Some can wait. Nevertheless, we need two miracles. First, to furnish a cruise ship on an extremely tight budget. Second, the stuff has to have the Look. Ordinary will not do.

Having no idea where to begin, a girl turns to her best friend: Google. Colorado Springs is the largest town nearby. "Used furniture." Presto! Platte Furniture pops up.

We skedaddle.

Platte did not disappoint. Divide and conquer. Eagle-eyes spots a wagon-wheel coffee table tucked out of sight and makes a beeline across the field of furniture to the store's back corner. The weathered wagon-wheel table is upheld by four massive hubs. Saved for the likes of us.

No doubt, contemporary homes have no need for such a piece. But we do! Oh, the stories. Gamblers and gunslingers. Stagecoach robberies. See the marks?

No doubt Wyatt Earp and Billy the Kid dug their spurs in this wheel. The real deal. Not no stinkin' imitation. Oh, the tales it will tell. "SOLD!"

Fingers gently glide over names etched in an old worn desktop. Infatuated, I fondle the sleek wooden flip seat and admire the black ornamental legs. "What a marvelous entry piece."

"Here's two student desks." The 1950s version.

"What would we do with those?"

"How about nightstands?" Now that's an outside-the-box thinker.

We're as giddy as kids in a candy store. "Look! A dainty vintage brass bedframe. How cool is that?!"

"Perfect! Oh, my! Isn't this wingback leather recliner great? The distressed texture. The color. Perfect." Flip the price tag and glee erupts, only one hundred twenty-five dollars.

"Hey babe, do you like this distressed turquoise sideboard? It could serve as our headboard!"

"How's that supposed to work? It's a sideboard." I quiz.

"Put the bed in the middle of the room."

Strange, but why not? "It'll be warmer than sleeping under the drafty window and against log walls as we experienced last night," the man of taste reasons.

I'm tellin' ya, he's a thinking machine.

"It's unexpected. I like it."

"Do you like this rich ebony highboy? Even though it's brand new, architecturally it's a great compliment to the headboard."

"It'll work."

Bouncing from one distressed piece to another, we find unbelievable prices and perfect fits for an old log cabin. We were over the moon.

"What about this tooled leather armchair?"

"I saw it. The seat is cracked!"

"It's not cracked. It's split."

"Potāto, potato. Have you seen such a piece? You cannot duplicate authentic patina. The medieval throne-esque piece is embellished with oversized nail heads, both oval and round. It's a one-of-a-kind statement piece for mere pennies."

"SOLD!"

A textured gray fainting couch catches my attention. Tufts were not what we had in mind, neither was new, nor gray. However, gray will soften all the natural wood and cream tones. Shoppers waffle before concluding, SOLD. It's perfect.

Vintage lamps? Yes! Not just one, but several. A photographer's lamp catches Mr. Budde's discerning eye. He rubs it and continues to rub. And continues.

"Slap him!"

"SOLD!"

"What about this camel saddle? Rustic is good. For what? A footstool? An extra seat?"

"We'll figure it out. It's cool. I want it." The discriminating man gets his way.

"Look at this pretty wicker mirror and shelves. They'll look great in the guest room. Not too big, just right."

"Ding, ding, ding! A snowshoe chair! A lowrider it is. Try it, luv."

"Perfect! Now that's a unique piece."

Stockers continue to unload a steady flow of gems onto the showroom floor. "I bet you've never seen a piece like this before, have you babe?" says the interior designer, pointing out the rustical teak dining table that only minutes ago was unloaded off the truck.

"The price tag is way too high."

"But look at it. It's made of old wagon wheel spokes and includes two spoked chairs. Who could resist? Luv, it's made for our front porch. We saved a ton of money. To pay more than we'd like on an item or two is fine. It all comes out in the wash."

"It's too expensive."

"Sooo, where else will you find such a piece?"

He caved.

All the pieces will live happily ever after in our little log cabin. Okay, in our not so little log cabin.

One works up a sweat spending all this money in a frenzy. A shopping spree orchestrated by the Lord. We found many VERY COOL items, all with the Look!

"Do you need a mattress?" the owner, Richard Kelly, asks, upselling his happy customers. "It's four weeks out for delivery on a mattress." He directs us to the options. "We'll take two queens. Firm, please."

"We don't usually furnish an entire house," Mr. Kelly says.

"You are today! Will you sharpen your pencil?" Mr. Budde asks.

Mr. Kelly grinds his pencil down to a stub. Forty-five-hundred dollars. Delivery included. We are ecstatic! And so was the shopkeeper.

All due to the prayers of a new friend.

Platte Furniture becomes our favorite stop to scout treasures. Never have we come close to the rare finds discovered that divine day.

But the Budde's always enjoy the hunt.

How'd we do? Sweet huh?

Inside the historic cabin

You Got This Vern!

Vern's got nothin' but time for fixin' stuff. Whenever work is involved, the two of us have taken a fond liking to slippin' into Vern and Vernette mode. Just for fun, play along. Allow every word to slooooowly roll off the tongue. Vern 'n' Vernette infuses charm 'n' character into a casual way of speakin'. English not hardly spoken as linguists intended.

Drives 'em crazy.

Embrace the brief alternative to reality. It's therapeutic.

Refurbishing an old cabin is like herding cats. Ya catch one and another suddenly breaks loose. But Vern 'n' Vernette are gettin' 'er done! Weeez showin' it some LOVE. An enormous job, the kind him was lookin' fer.

That fireplace needs more than a spit shine. Poof, watch a wad of cash go up in smoke. Better than asphyxiation I suppose.

Not to insult a child's creative touch, splattered wall texture might impress parents but falls short for Vern 'n' Vernette. That Vern will whack that weird texture right off them thar walls in nothin' flat. Yessiree, that's what him does, cleans up after others. Him does what others can't.

Him's good too.

The upstairs latrine needs attention. Hold the toilet paper roll! One level down dispenses a story fit for a king.

The fix-it list grows and grows and grows. Could take a lifetime. Unless ya play the lottery. Since we don't, Vern 'n' Vernette will have to get creative. It's what they do. It's how they roll.

Life just ain't all about work. Vern will tell ya what him's gonna do and just how slow him's gonna do it. After all, porch sittin' time is important.

Come, sit a spell. Wave at all the beautiful people drivin' by. The porch is a mighty fine place to experience time travel.

Do ya hear that sound? AH, it's work callin'. You got this Vern! Get busy.

King of NO

Without hesitation, the word NO simply glides off Mr. Budde's lips.

With a dash of finesse applied, one's no can be converted into a yes. Shhhhh, it'll ruin his image.

The decorator envisions a more western ambience. "How about a whiskey barrel? A hammered copper sink? A wagon wheel chandelier?" She claims, "these items will enhance and elevate the cabin's historical value."

Fast 'n' furious the response flies from the king's lips, "NO! It's too big, too heavy, and too expensive."

Give the man kudos, he can put his foot down when called upon to do so. Upon the cabin closing, his wife insisted, "you must love the cabin for what it is," as the purchase price far surpassed our intended purse strings.

Well, that didn't last long.

Before you know it, we're in search of wall sconces to replace the out of context southwest sconces in the great room. Old lanterns are a much better fit. Richard spots the perfect sconces on Craigslist.

To drive across town in a blizzard for a fifty-dollar purchase is not unreasonable. We're headed to the cabin anyway.

"Luv, I'll wait in the car."

Moments later, a knock on the passenger window, "Mrs. Budde, you must come see!"

"Really?" Most unhappy to trudge through two feet of snow.

"Really. Come see!" Mr. Budde persists.

The underdressed babe follows the excited hunter into the garage.

Piles of cabin-esque items consume the entire garage. Items like, a wagon wheel chandelier, a whiskey keg transformed into a vanity, coordinating wall sconces, a mica light bar, and so much more. What about a hammered copper sink? Inquiring minds want to know.

"Do you have a copper sink?"

The fella navigates to the corner, digs through stacks of stuff from the abyss and retrieves two, that's right, two hammered copper sinks!

"Like these?" he says, waving the sinks overhead with pride.

"Yes! Like those." I'm ecstatic! "Do you happen to have a faucet in that magical abyss of yours?"

Back to the abyss he digs. Extraction happens. "Like this?"

"Yes! Like that!" Amazingly, the faucet matches the cabin's other bathroom faucets. Only God. Redemption has come!

This contractor stashed a houseful of cabin accessories in the garage. He's overloaded with priceless gems gutted from a former Avalanche player's home. Prestigious, right?

Mica light sconces and light bar are added to the stash.

Beyond thrilled! I love when God shows His favor. But Mr. Budde must agree. He does. How can he deny God's provision?

The king of NO reverses his response.

"Yes!" Decorator scores!

Doesn't the chandelier make a grand statement?

Freshly improved upper level

Notice the bank vault door masterfully duplicated by the King of NO. Impressive, right? It's what him does.

Don't assume a stash of cash is behind that fancy vault door. It's the attic entrance.

There comes a time when God's goodness just flows. It's called *favor*.

The old painting in the photo was picked up for a song off Craigslist. The art style resembles the work of Allen True, an artist of the 1930s whose murals abound in Colorado's State capital. At the time of purchase, we had no idea the painting was a perfect representation of our cabin's builder and entrepreneurial drover, JJ Sease.

We assumed JJ used horses, as many photos in the valley show horses pulling wagons. But "NO", oxen were JJ's work animal of choice. The unexpected weaves together.

That man of mine is a serious shopper. But nothing compares to God's favor. Nothing.

Tales to Tell

History knocked at our door, one fine day. Fit as a fiddle in his eighties, a descendant of JJ Sease found himself standing on the front porch of history. Holy Moses! The old guy had tales to tell! His mama was born and raised in our prized possession.

JJ built the cabin in the 1800s. Best we can figure around 1874.

Bob reminisced childhood stories.

"My grandpappy was sittin' on this porch sippin' tea when an Indian with a herd of horses stopped by and asked if the horses could use his waterin' hole. 'Help yourself,' grandpappy offered.

"Days later, an Indian grandpappy knew stopped by and asked if he'd seen a herd of horses?"

"Yes. A day or so ago."

"Those are my horses. Which direction did they go?"

JJ pointed east and warned, "They went that away. Don't go after them. There's way more of them than with you."

"The Indian thanked him and took off east. Several days later JJ's Indian friend stopped by with his herd of horses and a pole of scalps."

YIKES! The tales of yesteryear.

Made-up stories about our wagon wheel coffee table were put to shame. We now have *real* stories, not just fables. Stories of the valley's own notorious rustlers.

Months later, twenty inmates from the local prison gathered below our front porch. The fellas just completed a hard day of fire mediation. Curiously they asked insignificant questions about the cabin like, "Where did you get the furniture on the porch?"

Why talk furnishings when this place oozes with fascinating stories?

The storyteller redirected the conversation. Prisoners were intrigued. Some jumped out of the caravan to catch an earful.

"The cabin's builder, JJ Sease, was a transporter of goods. He was traveling on the desert flats when robbed by a cattle rustler named Juan Mace. Juan stole everything from JJ. Stripped of his goods, JJ walked to town, rounded up a posse, and hunted Mace down into this valley formally known as Mace's Hole."

Everything taken was found.

According to JJ's great-grandson, Bob, "JJ hung Juan Mace and shot his two sons." Although the valley's version is slightly different.

Inmates' jaws dropped. Their eyes grew big as saucers.

It occurred to me the audience to whom I was speaking were all convicts, so I reminded them, "Justice was swift in the 1800s."

Oh, the tales to be told over the past hundred and fifty years. If these walls could talk. To hear the skinny from family members who lived here. History comes alive.

PRICELESS.

Travel to the year 1923, the late Colorado Governor Orman's son purchased this stunning log cabin from JJ. Governor Orman (1901–1903), a successful businessman in his day, left a true legacy in the area.

Mr. Orman's company was responsible for laying train tracks all over this entire region.

Early part of the century, gifts adorned the cabin's hand-hewed logs. A chief's headdress and treasures from local and distant Indian tribes alike hung from these logs. The collection of historic treasures now rotates at Colorado State University's extension in Pueblo.

Hours untold were spent removing buckets of nails protruding from these logs. Surprises lurk. Be cautious.

Out of the blue, on multiple occasions, members of the Orman Clan stopped by to reminisce about their family homestead of forty years. It's fun to experience a guided tour through the history of your old place.

The crooked rail-tie fence surrounding the property tips its hat to the railroad titans.

Thanks for indulging me before slapping me down.

Holy Smoke!

"Mr. Budde, will you still love this cabin if it takes every last dime we have?" I asked Richard at closing.

Enthusiastically he responded, "OH, YES!"

A few years following the purchase of the historic project, I grew rather cranky. To maintain two clingy and needy properties takes a toll.

Richard pours time and money, lots of money, into the cabin while cranky stays behind.

Feeling the pinch, Ms. Cranky storms into God's complaint department with a few choice words. Good thing the door is always open. God is never too busy. Never chastises. Just listens to the rampage. Occasionally, He provides insight or answers. Mostly I just rail. Like today.

"God, this cabin is sucking us dry. It's a constant drain. We can't afford to go anywhere or do anything."

You know the whine routine. Cranky suffers a severe case.

Relieved after expressing my complaint to the Almighty, my husband returns from his rendezvous with his newfound love, the cabin.

Richard's warm embrace, welcoming smile, comforting hugs, kisses, and extensive rubbing tells a different story.

"Hon, I had the most surprising dream."

"Do tell. I'm all ears." With coffee in hand, off to the vee-randa we trot. Snuggle in for Richard's dreamy story.

"In my dream, I was sitting on the cabin's front porch. A sleek black SUV slowly drives past, you know, the telltale signs of a realtor. A lady stopped, got out, and asked if I wanted to sell the cabin. Of course, I said 'NO, it's not for sale.'"

"But I did offer to let them see it. The couple gawked about. Before leaving the realtor asked, '*If* it were for sale, how much would you want?' I threw out a ridiculous amount, one point seven million!"

"A few days later the realtor came and offered one and a half million. I was stunned. 'Sold!'"

"Then I woke up and heard, 'they would have paid one point seven.'"

"HOLY SMOKES! ARE YOU KIDDING?"

Here Ms. Cranky whines about budget concerns, and the Lord gives Mr. Budde a phenomenal dream to the contrary. A serious slap-down! Knocks self-pity out cold.

Whining is replaced by profitability of the extraordinary kind.

Without reservation, Vern 'n' Vernette continue to improve the property. After all, there is a windfall coming. With great joy, we pour love and money into the glorious project. At the time of this dream, that price truly was inconceivable.

And Ms. Cranky thought we'd do well to merely recoup our investment.

God is SOOOO MUCH BIGGER.

The dream did trigger the question: Would we really sell? Even for one-point seven million?

Today, we both say no. We love the cabin and community too much. Tomorrow's answer could be different. We're flexible like that.

When real estate prices escalated, one point seven million approached a strong reality, that was before the market took a serious nosedive. Did we miss our window?

The market will circle back around. It always does.

Heart 2 Heart

Who'd expect the bib overall-wearing, white-haired codger to be such a fashionista? The evidence speaks for itself. A celebrity of sorts. Compliments and admiration flock the geezer sporting his retirement uniform.

Step away from the city for an entirely different lifestyle.

Perched on the porch in his patinaed rockin' chair, the Fashionista waves at folks passing. Squawking turkeys, blue jays, black pointy-eared squirrels, an occasional herd of buck or a doe and her spotted fawns wander by to entertain the fashionista. Frequently the neighbors stop to chat.

"Howdy, neighbor! Come, sit a spell. This old man needs some porch sittin' time after working five sweltering days on the tractor." Mr. Budde removes his straw hat and wipes his sweaty brow.

"Ahh, the breeze feels so good. You know, a couple years ago I flat-out couldn't do this 'n' that."

Simply, "Do what?" the neighbor inquires.

"Climb on and off a tractor in all this heat. I was good for nothing," says Mr. Budde. "I'd plumb run out of energy. Thought it was the meds at first."

"Was it?" the neighbor asks.

"No, not at all. The doctor poked and prodded, then got excited listening to my heart. They ran an EKG. Hullabaloo broke out as it flashed, popped, and sputtered out my heartbeat. The doc scribbled on his notepad and told me, 'I'll prescribe several medications.' Emphatically, I told him, 'I don't want to take all those drugs. Let's talk options.' 'Look, I'm just trying to keep you alive,' the doctor snapped."

"That must have been scary."

"If that news doesn't make your heart skip a beat, I don't know what will," retorts Mr. Budde. "The Doc insisted, 'Let the cardiologist take it from here. You need to be seen right away. These drugs will keep you alive until then.'" Mr. Budde leans toward neighbor, "Great words of comfort, huh?"

He continues, "I confess, this old geezer didn't waste any time to see a specialist. They hitched up that contraption. Wires and sticky tabs all over my hairy chest. The CNA ignites the space-age device for takeoff. Again, it flashes, pops, and prints the exciting results. In a tizzy, the staff spun about in a whirlwind." Richard pauses to wave at the cyclist passing by before continuing, "The physician's assistant told me, 'It's unusual to catch A-fib in action! It happens so infrequently.'"

Fashionista's bride delivers tall mason jars of freshly brewed iced tea and joins the conversation. "That Mr. Budde is hardly ordinary. No wonder his heart action is captured every time. He's special like that."

Inquiring minds want to know. "What is A-fib?"

Miracle man slooowly sips his tea and takes a deep breath. "Simply put, the heart's upper chambers are out of time with the lower chambers. To experience the whirlwind was much like watching a Laurel and Hardy comedy routine."

"Did the drugs work?" neighbor asks.

"Depends on the expectation. Meds certainly slowed down my heart. Exhaustion just felt different. Who knows. Maybe they did. After all, I am alive."

"How did you deal with the exhaustion?"

"Five-hour naps."

"That's not living!" exclaims the neighbor.

"It was nearly impossible to get anything done. My life stopped. They wanted to do a cardioversion. Not without research, I balked."

"What is a cardioversion?"

"A procedure where they kill you, then resurrect you! Case in point is a guy on YouTube who awakens during the procedure. Watch it. He shot straight up! How's that for comforting?"

"Gasp!!"

"Horrifically hysterical, assuming it's not you. Now, why would I willfully participate in such an experiment?"

His sweetheart interrupts to calm the delusional portrayal, "It is simply a heart reboot, much like rebooting your laptop. Takes nearly the same amount of time too. Presto! The man looks no worse for the wear." Doting over her handsome fashionista with a smouch and a wink. "Luv, tell neighbor, if you felt any different?"

"YES! YES, I did."

"Walks were restored." His bride adds, "For a week anyway, before lightning struck again. Prior to the onset of A-fib, this man ran circles around me. Richard's walk slowed to a crawl."

"Oh, we prayed, how we prayed, yet nothing changed."

"Life passed in slow motion. Plans, dreams, aspirations placed on hold as the tired one longed for energy to dream again."

Neighbor wants to know, "Did you pester God for healing?"

"Every day I told the Lord, you gotta heal me. This is a nightmare. I can't live like this. It's horrible. I've had a bellyful. You've got to fix my heart. So yes, I pestered God. He tells me, He's my healer. Either it's true or it's not."

Neighbor struggles to wrap his head around divine healing. "How do you know if it's God's will for you to be healed?"

"By His stripes I am healed, the Word tells me in Isaiah 53:5. That's ME He's talking to. Not someday or hopefully. He says, 'I am healed!' All His gifts, like love, grace, and salvation are free for ALL to receive TODAY." Passionately Richard explains before continuing his story.

"The frequent occurrence plays out at the cardiologists. You know the routine. Out came the EKG, wires, sticky tabs, and such. The physician assistant gets all lathered up in a frenzy."

Neighbor is stunned.

"You get used to it. Except the time the doctor informed me, 'Mr. Budde, you are in a constant state of A-fib, not merely an occasional event.' For the first time, endless exhaustion made sense. This old ticker flutters all the time. Doc announced, 'Next up, a cardiac ablation!'"

Mrs. Budde adds, "He was not happy."

"I informed the doc, 'NO WAY!' I was determined not to allow the doctor do as he pleased."

"Mr. Budde, what is a cardio ablation?" neighbor asks.

"They burn scars on your heart to regulate your heartbeat."

"Does it work?"

"Not for my brother it didn't. The doctor told me, 'that's as good as it gets then. Unless you'd consider a pacemaker.'" All worked up, Mr. Budde continues. "No way! My brother went down this identical path, and he is no better off. NO WAY! I'm not going through that for the same result."

Neighbor compassionately responds, "I'm sorry to hear."

"Why let doctor's proclamations seal my fate?! My prayers are relentless. 'Lord, this is not living. You've got to fix my heart!' Nearly two years have passed since the fluttering began. Then out of the blue on a lazy Sunday afternoon, I was lying in bed here at the cabin when I heard, *'You're healed.'*"

"I wanted him to go get checked, but he wouldn't. He's stubborn like that."

"Luv, my scheduled cardiac appointment followed several months later. That was good enough. Out came the EKG, wires, sticky tabs, and such. You know the routine."

"Want more tea?" asks Mrs. Budde.

"She takes such good care of me." Mr. Budde dotes.

"Then the cardiologist entered the exam room with his stethoscope draped around his neck." Mr. Budde demonstrates, "Doc leaned in and listened here and there, front and back, then inquisitively repeated the process. 'Hmm, your heart sounds perfectly normal,' commented the skeptic."

Neighbor is surprised too.

"For an old geezer, my energy level is above average. Many are shocked by my agility, ability, strength, and remarkable good looks. It must be the company I keep," Mr. Budde directs attention to his much, much younger blushing bride running her fingers through his white hair.

Laughter erupts.

"Yes, yes, of course that's it, Luv."

In the Genes

My doctor relentlessly pressures me to comply with orthodox medical procedures. I'm very leery as several family members have suffered repercussions at the hands of modern medicine.

Ms. Leery doesn't want a fistfight every time she goes to the doctor as she tries hard not to transgress.

An annoyed prayer is muttered, as the vehemently opposed patient heads to the doctor. "If this continues, I'll switch doctors or… or… or worse! Lord, help me control my bad self and handle this situation with grace."

Of course, the anticipated question arrives. "Is there a reason you didn't follow through with the prescribed procedure?"

"Yes."

Silence follows. Eyes fish for an explanation. Pondering on how to reply.

"It's in the genes," Ms. Leery states emphatically.

Silently Doc waits for details. He's not moving off the topic.

"My daddy was a genius. He didn't trust doctors. As kids we thought he was a fool. It's in the genes." I shrug.

With a blank look, the doctor turns, advances toward his flat screen and quietly states, "Your daddy was no fool."

He might have thought this curly cotton top is hard of hearing, but I am not. I heard. No more did we tangle over medical choices. And nobody got hurt.

The Christmas Grinch

The Christmas season is tough on an old babe who stands all day. It's just hours away from a ten-day vacay. Yahoo!

Just thinking about our last stop makes me salivate. Number three is the BOMB! Pork and avocado burrito smothered in Christmas chili, a chili relleno, a chicken taco served on a crisp homemade shell is to die for. Add authentic refried beans and it's like no other—kisses to all the deliciousness. Our favorite Pueblo restaurant: Mia Ranchito II.

Two events will converge while on vacation: to brainstorm remodeling ideas for the upstairs bathroom and plan next year's annual Christmas gathering. It's our year to host. To avoid last year's airport shut down, for an alternative July was chosen. PERFECT!

Imagine twinkling lights strung about the wraparound-porch and a campy gift exchange. The Christmas tree aglow! It'll be SOOOO festive. Roasted marshmallows and carols over the summer's open bonfire. Under the stars the storyteller could expound the greatest story ever told.

Exhale a sigh of relief. Another stunning Colorado sunset goes unnoticed. AWE at last. In a land where time stops.

Ol' Blue, we fondly call our Subaru Outback, follows the yellow lines down the highway. Up the tree-lined drive we fly. Fresh pine floats upon the crisp mountain night air mixed with a hint of firewood. Take a breath. Isn't it divine?

"Welcome to the cabin." A dimly lit storybook log cabin set amongst the trees, admired every time we drive up the drive.

Mundanely, I insert the key into the backdoor, turn the knob, and step in. Greeted by the unexpected sound of Niagara Falls.

Panic strikes.

Speculations rise. *Has the hot water tank blown up?* Hearts stop. Adrenaline kicks in. Plowing over each other, Richard and I rush down the hallway toward the source. We ski through a river flowing over pristine hardwood floors, barely noting pools gurgling beneath the drywall.

The family historian whips out her phone to document the event sloshing through the primary bedroom and bathroom, abruptly stopping at the laundry room door.

If I turn on the lights to enter, will I get electrocuted? I don't know. This I do know, water and electricity don't mix. It could get ugly.

Mr. Budde spins a U-turn and sprints to shut off the water. Never has he moved so fast!

The family historian captures the disaster in real time, posting on social media. Records are good to have. One never knows what the future holds.

Everything is soaked. Realization sets in. Disheartened reality swirls in my head, *We have a five-thousand-dollar deductible.*

Vern has poured TONS of hours and dollars transforming this place. The hallway underwent a HUGE transformation. Nail holes filled. Loose wallpaper repaired. Terracotta gone. Walls now painted string of pearls. Sconces changed. Now a soggy mess. Ruined. Hardwood floors cupped. Destroyed!

"It's too late tonight to cleanup. Let's wait 'til morning," the wise tired soul insists before his attention shifts to: *why is it so cold?* Chilly is normal, but not this chilly, at least not since replacing the furnace three years earlier.

"OMG! Thirty-four degrees!" Mr. Budde turns up the thermostat. "Heat should kick on quickly," he assures his frost-bitten wife.

But it doesn't. Absolutely nothing happens.

Days before Christmas, subzero temperatures covered the state of Colorado. No reason for concern, as we were proud owners of a new furnace.

Exhausted, Mr. Budde decides, "I'll call the repair guys in the morning."

Heart sick, we drag our overwhelmed bodies to the guest room, turn on the space heater and crank the electric blanket to broil.

Wakeup call brightly streamed through the skylight. The sun's welcomed warmth takes the edge off what lies ahead.

Coffee is a must. Oh, that's right, we have no water. UGH!

Discovery begins with morning light.

I'll do my best to explain. It'll be tough to keep up with the cabin's convoluted floorplan. Float over the main bedroom's raspberry carpet. Now dive into the saturated swimming hole, known as the ensuite. Jump over the floating threshold. Be careful. Watch the narrow step. Whew! It's a job navigating. But you nailed the landing. Behold, the soggy laundry room floor.

Would you looky there. Right there. On the floor. The culprit. The hot water shut off valve. Blown to smithereens. Smack dab through the threads!

Like a geyser hot water shot out from the half inch water pipe, not the tank as assumed last night. No tank could keep up with such a demand.

Fortunately, my vintage sewing machine was saved. But the dresser and table are ruined as are my stash of *Cody* books.

Break time! We need water. We need coffee. We need help. Around the corner is the Fire department. Water containers in tow, off we go.

Brew makes everything better. So does flushing toilets.

An S.O.S. is shot into the world of social media, hoping to discover some kind of redeeming value beyond endless ads. Our hood instantaneously delivers. Fans, heaters, and a water extraction tools knock at our door. Everything needed to suck up, dry out, and warm up a cavernous iceberg.

Impressive, right? Electric fans, kerosene heater, log fireplace, all roar at full tilt.

After walking into an unheated cabin three years earlier, we replaced the forty-year-old untrustworthy furnace.

That outage prepared us for a powerless environment. But NEVER did it prepare us for frozen pipes! Or a flood.

Vern tears into soggy walls and manages HVAC and plumbing repairmen while the much younger Vernette works her heinie off, extracting flood water and tearing out drenched carpet in the bathroom. We scoop buckets and more buckets of water from the laundry room's cavernous well head.

Every three hours day and night, Vern or Vernette stoke the fireplace insert. Who needs sleep? Superheroes don't sleep. Sleep is highly overrated in crisis.

Six days later, we remain stuck in a chilly log cabin. I know. I know.

Cranky and tired, ready to slap somebody, anybody at this point, possibly the one I love most. "Babe, I've got to get some rest before returning to work," leaving behind an equally tired and cranky husband to stoke the fire.

It took TEN, I repeat, TEN LONG COLD nights before that miserable lame furnace was repaired. It's no wonder he's sick!

PTSD subsides a little bit. The cabin dries out as best it could in the dead of winter with closed windows.

Much discussion was had over insurance. Mr. Budde is quite definitive, "If we file a claim, we'll get canceled. Insurance is waaay too difficult to get in the forest. NO! I'll do all the work myself."

"Maybe we can get assistance from the manufacturer. It just ain't right, for you to do all the repairs." Disgruntled I stand.

While the man awaits the repair, I became well acquainted with the manufacturer's customer service department. Information flowed. Including a restoration estimate.

The manufacturer's response was encouraging.

Weeks transpired before the death blow, "due to the age of the furnace, they will NOT cover any consequential damages."

WRONG ANSWER! *I think not.* I'll reach out to the CEO. Mercy! Talk about wallerin' in the dough!

Upper management pounced on their customers with unsolicited property advice. WOW! Not a response I saw coming. SHAZAM!! Outraged! Slap that arrogant bulldog! The Grinch stole our Christmas and now refuses to pay. Unacceptable! We'll see you in court! It just ain't right.

Pay close attention…

To the simple details

of the Grinch that stole Christmas

2022

The Grinch's name

is ▮▮▮▮▮▮.

A three-year-old furnace blew out its brain.

At a most inopportune time.

Temperatures fell, pipes froze, then burst

leaving an empty 36-thousand-dollar purse.

"File an insurance claim,"
The Grinch proclaimed!
"When a faulty lame furnace is to blame?"
Preposterous!
Are they insane?

It was the beginning of a "normal" day when I hear,
"Don't be discouraged, Mrs. Budde, I have your back."
So simple. So profound.

Deliverance

On the heels of a twenty-one day fast, an Encounter Night was hosted at the church. Come expecting God to move! I was and He did. When floating about the room, praying for people, an arm ushered me to the front. Prayer warriors surrounded a very upset young lady, sharing her sister's gut-wrenching situation.

In broken English, Carolina shares an unbelievable story: "My sister was abducted. She lives in a very rough part of Mexico. We posted photos of Fernanda on Facebook, asking if anyone had seen her.

"'You shouldn't have done that,' her abductors threatened."

Carolina was visibly distraught over not knowing if Fernanda was dead or alive. A handful of intercessors circled her and began to pray.

A vision, which I'm not inclined to have, came to me. In the middle of a large empty room stood a young lady clothed in fire, not consuming but a protective fire, like Moses experienced at the burning bush. The room's prison bars held the young lady captive. Barred gates suddenly opened.

The prayer warrior pressed in according to the vision on behalf of Fernanda. It wasn't complicated or lengthy.

"Lord, may those who kidnapped this young woman see the fire and know it's the presence of God upon Fernanda and release her immediately!"

The sister cried, "If only I knew she was alive."

Curly cotton top wanted to slap her! Instead, I sternly proclaimed, "I don't pray pretty little prayers in hopes. I prayed what I saw. Receive it or not." And walked off in a huff.

We want a miracle. We are desperate. Yet we resist. Why? It chaps my hide.

The following weekend was spent at the cabin. I don't recall thinking anymore about the vision. Truth be told, I probably was still annoyed.

Ten days later, a conference began. Three different people from the prayer circle came up and asked, "Have you heard?"

"Heard what?" the curious one responded.

"SHE'S FREE! They set Fernanda free! The head of the gang told her, 'I don't know what god you pray to. We were a fine-oiled machine until you came along. But since you've arrived, we've experienced nothing but chaos. You need to leave.' They opened the door and escorted her out!"

Overcome with God's goodness, I wept.

Inquiring minds want to know: "How is Fernanda doing?"

"She's stuck in the tragedy. My sister is afraid to go outside. She's so sad."

"No doubt the trauma was severe. I will continue to pray for her." Which I do, but with no apparent change.

Some feed fear by reliving an event.

No good can come of this.

"Tell Fernanda to stop focusing on her abduction," I tell Carolina. "Focus on God's deliverance."

A month later, we head to San Diego for a boat show. Make it a family affair. Joining us, my sister, Denise, yachty Kevin, a.k.a. brother-n-love, and their two daughters hobnob with impersonators of the rich 'n' famous.

Our first night in San Diego, I have a dream.

This dream involved Denise's group of believers from Red Seal Ministries. In the dream, we were all together praying. I heard myself praying, "Fernanda, Fernanda, hear the word of the Lord." Odd, as I've never prayed in this manner before. After the unusual introduction, powerful prayer warriors take over. Trauma surgeons in the spirit intercede for Fernanda. The type you want in your corner when PTSD symptoms rule.

That was the end of my dream.

This should come as no surprise but on Tuesday Red Seal Ministries meets for dinner and we'll be there. Dinner is luscious. God stories are shared. People get healed, but nothing like seen in the dream.

Being flexible, I shake it off. *It's okay,* I justify. After all, God gave the dream. Who am I to force the dream into reality?

It was a couple of weeks before my sis reconnected with Red Seal and asked them to intercede for Fernanda's trauma. They did. I wasn't there, but they are highly effective at casting off trauma.

It's been about six weeks since Red Seal intercessors prayed. I'm compelled to check on Fernanda. The next day I beeline it for a status report. The congregation is large. One can easily disappear in the crowd. Not certain what Carolina even looks like. This could be a hunt.

"God lead me; certainly, she's here."

Toward the end of service, in the dim light, I spot who I think is Carolina chatting. The inquisitive one waits her turn. With anticipation, "How is Fernanda doing?"

"She is doing great! She is happy. She is back to living life."

My heart is overwhelmed. Delivered not once, but twice! Maybe someday, Denise and I will meet Fernanda. Maybe.

Not Hardly
The
END

In Conclusion

Hopefully, *Talk To Me God, Before I Slap Somebody!* was worthy of your time.

It's tough to behave, particularly when annoyed. Frequently, I bite my tongue. To practice kindness is the best defense. Makes it easier when I get a hankering to slap somebody.

My antidote: Don't bow to anger, bitterness, offenses, or hatred. Trust me, they come knockin'. Don't let them in. It's not easy to let go. Nothing worth doing is easy.

Sidenote: unforgiveness chains us to the very person we won't forgive. Roots dig deep, contaminating our souls. Even if that person deserves to be punished, by not forgiving them, we bear the repercussions. Not them. Just sayin'.

Life is full of hard choices.

I've remained free as a bird, well, other than being muzzled and silenced by some. Occasionally, I shake from captivity! FREEDOM is beautiful. Murderous rage is ferocious and deadly. Fortunately, I've never had to beat it back down.

Someone told me dyslexia is a gift. I'd never thought of it as such. However, the fact that I don't quickly catch on, has caused me to seek God. For which I'm extremely grateful. God knew what he was doing when He "gifted" me with such special traits.

If you think *Talk to Me God, Before I Slap Somebody!* was grand? Try *Cody, Life Lessons Inspired by My Spirited Mare.*

Hope you received more than entertainment.

If you dare, pray the prayer below, it could change your life.

Lord,

Give me eyes to see your outrageous love towards me,

no matter what I've done.

Help me to believe. Break off unbelief.

Bathe me in your divine presence,

and transformational power.

Bring revelation of who you are.

Cause me to recognize

Your divine intervention.

Open my ears to clearly hear your voice.

In Jesus' precious name,

Amen.

Acknowledgements

To God,

For the memory recall of His divine interventions in my life and spurring me on to tell them.

Mr. Budde,

May your sacrifice of cuddle and foot rubbing for the sake of *Talk to Me God, Before I Slap Somebody!* be greatly rewarded. You're the BEST proofreader, thought-provoker, gifted assistant a girl could have. You slay me!

My Friends,

Whose real names weave authenticity into the stories. Also, for the part you played in my life. YOU are a treasure.

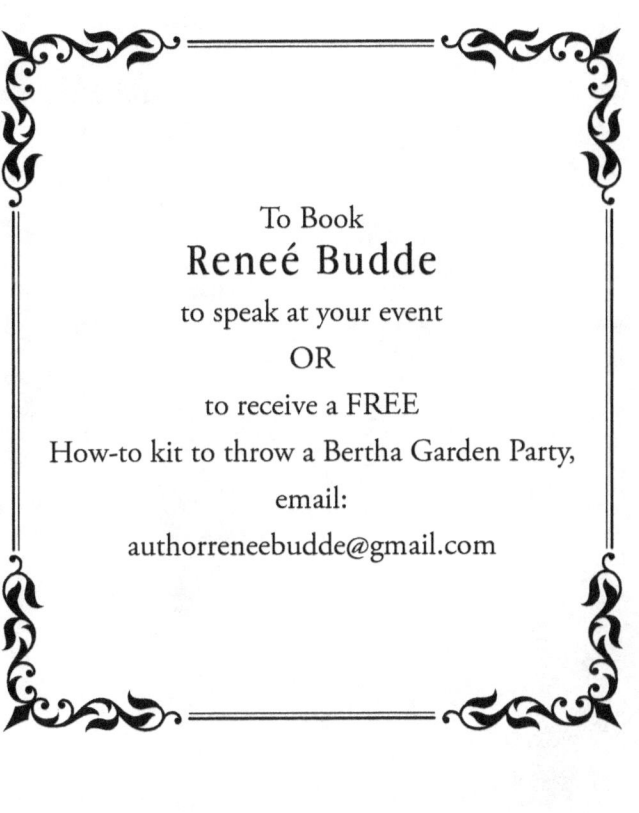

To Book
Reneé Budde
to speak at your event

OR

to receive a FREE

How-to kit to throw a Bertha Garden Party,

email:

authorreneebudde@gmail.com